The Real Jazz Old and New

The

Real Jazz Old and New

Written and illustrated by

STEPHEN LONGSTREET

LOUISIANA STATE UNIVERSITY PRESS

BY STEPHEN LONGSTREET

Travel

Last Man Around the World
The Last Man Comes Home
Chico Goes to the Wars
The World Revisited

Personal History

Nine Lives with Grandfather
The Sisters Liked Them Handsome
The Boy in the Model-T

Novels

Decade
The Sound of an American
Three Days (Gettysburg)
The Pedlocks
The Beach House
The Lion at Morning

Plays

High Button Shoes
Free World Theatre
(collaboration with Thomas Mann and Arch Oboler)

Motion Pictures

The Jolson Story
Uncle Harry
Stallion Road
Greatest Show on Earth

Library of Congress Card Catalog Number: 56-11355.
Manufactured in the U.S.A. by William Byrd Press.

To the memory of two of the best of all jazzmen . . .

Charles "Buddy" Bolden
Joseph "King" Oliver

Table of Contents

Introduction

I didn't *write* this book. I *heard* it. Almost all of it was told to me by many jazzmen over a period of years when I was drawing and painting the jazz life in New Orleans and New York and Chicago and Los Angeles. The jazzmen of the stone age of jazz are dying off fast, and this book is a record of their talk, of the things they had to say about jazz and its inventors. Some few of them were educated enough to have been to college and most of them had learned about life the hard way, but what they had to say was in most cases important, and when they were gone their knowledge and their comments would be gone with them. They were not writers, and few of them were famous. But they had been there, and they had grown up with it. So this book is theirs, several hundred of them whom I listened to and whose words I put down in my sketch books.

This is a collection of their words, of voices and of sounds. It is *not* a history of jazz in the formal sense, and it certainly is *not* an appraisal of jazz from the critics' viewpoint.

I have done my part of making this book by selecting a part of the thousands of drawings I have made in the jazz joints, among the jazzmen, and in trying to fit together the voices of the jazzmen under chapter headings and under topics that make this an honest journey to jazz that can no longer be made, as most of the voices here heard are gone. I have left it in their words. This should be a book of fun and fury and sounds and taste of what jazz was, and is. I don't know of another book like it—that lets the jazzmen tell their own story in their own words. I have tried to show in black and white what it looked like and felt.

In 1768, at Drury Lane Theater, in London, in a comic opera, *The Padlock,* a Negro slave, Mungo, sings:

What a terrible life I am led
A dog has it better
That's sheltered and fed
Night and day it's the same
My pain is their game—
Me wish to the Lord me was dead.

Whatever's to be done
Poor black must run—
Mungo here, Mungo there,
Mungo everywhere.
Above and below—
Sirah come, Sirrah go.
Do so and do so
Me wish to the Lord me was dead.

It wasn't a Negro song written by Negroes, but was one of the first Negro themes on record and had the true feel from which the blues were to come, and from the blues, the classic jazz. And from jazz, a great many books. This is one of them.

More nonsense has been written about jazz than any subject except, perhaps, romantic love. This book hopes to add as little non-sense to the subject as it can. There is a jazz language, a way of talking and saying it that is personal and private to the jazzman and his world. You will find a lot of that language here, but this book is not all writ-ten in pure jazz language. It's hard to say after all the years that have gone into the making of this book just what it is. It's easier to put down what it is not. It isn't the official, definite history of anything. Jazz may someday have such a history, perhaps in a century. This book does not try to decide between those who see in jazz a good solid-knit folk music, and those who claim for it a big place as really great modern music, new and ready to do things as important, as, say, Mozart or Wagner or Stravinsky; this book has opinions, puts down a lot of facts, but it begs that big question. It's too soon to answer. It thinks jazz is music, but also explains why some people think it isn't. Mostly, this book tries to get down to what has so far often failed to appear about jazz in writing: the smell of the real thing, the mood and marrow, the blood and misery, the pleasure and ache of the jazz world. And the people who are in it.

It is a serious study and it treats jazz in a serious way. But, like jazz itself, it has tried to remain in its own backyard and get some fun, some of the fine feeling and some of the deep blue of jazz itself, into these pages. Reading about this music, frankly, is not to understand it fully. The perfect jazz book, besides the text, and the drawings and paintings, would have to hold in its index a pocket of about fifty recordings of the music that is the prime and basic stuff of jazz. Such a list—and no one of its followers would agree as to just what fifty sides to include—would take jazz from the church hymn turned blues, to the early work of Charles Buddy Bolden (if it exists on wax) through the whole Storyville era when jazz grew up in the canhouses of New Orleans, when King Oliver and Louie Armstrong were moving into Chicago, and when the music of Dixieland was making its part of jazz history. It would, perhaps, find room for Bix's *In A Mist,* and some of the newer experiments; stuff liked, or condemned, in bebop and cool jazz. It would leave out the concertos in pseudo-jazz form that aren't jazz, and most of the European stuff that is called concert jazz but isn't real jazz either.

Years of study and hard work went into this book, which shouldn't impress anyone as to its merits, but at least give it a deeper meaning than the usual casual approach to jazz. Old jazzmen are forgetful or great liars and so, in talking to them as to dates and titles, as to bands and music, it has always to be taken with a little doubt. If there are legends here, they are labeled as such—not as facts. The facts are here, too. Care has been taken to check dates, names, spellings, but in such a confused world as jazz, neglected and unrecorded (even if not unsung) errors will creep it.

In the end jazz remains a lot of fun, and a little sadness, a collection of music certainly original and American, and if some of the fun, the sadness and the music gets through and adds up here, the author will feel rewarded for what has been a very exciting part of anyone's life.

Almost every word in this book came from the memory of old jazzmen. When I quote them directly I put their words in quotes. When I distill their talk and connect it I have often retained their way of saying it. They may sound too lyrical and too excited, but rather than tone them down and lose something I have stuck to their own words. At the end of the book will be found details as to when and how the material for each chapter was collected, and notes that explain certain details.

Of the many people who helped with the collecting of this material and the editing of this book I want to thank and list the following. The late Mac Hedrick, who knew more about jazz, its people and its history than any human being I ever met, and who read through the early form of this book and set up several of the most important meetings that collected the best parts of this history. Montez Tjaden who led the author through New Orleans and the city of Washington where the last forms of the old jazz still existed, and whose aid in these cities went beyond the call of duty. James Welton who was playing Dixieland in Chicago in 1912 and whose union card is still in good standing, whose knowledge of all music is as great as his skill with recording machines and tape rolls and playbacks and editing. Charles E. Washburn owner of the Coast Record Company who can find almost any side you want to hear, or cut a new version of it. Milt Gross, now gone from us, whose knowledge of Harlem and its music in the old days was learned in the old newspaper days and whose ear for language was amazing, as his own printed work shows. Samuel Fuller, now a motion picture director who once also followed the beat. Charles Grayson, novelist and editor who grew up on the coast and knew the history of jazz there almost from the first blue note. James Cain, also an author, for some talks of music during the Civil War. Teddy Dale, who works on radio and television conducting and composing and arranging, and whose total recall of almost all music was better than a filing system. Red Nichols when I worked with him, writing a radio series. Howard Blake of show business. Lura Wallace of the Beverly Hills Library who gave me the clues to many forgotten items. Scott O'Dell of the Los Angeles *Mirror-News,* the best literary editor I ever worked for, who helped with many books. Henry Simon of Simon & Schuster whose first love is music. Agnes O'Malley Marx, historian of early film music. Harry Kaufman, concert piano player, for much advice. The late Joseph Johnston of Los Angeles City College, for whom I taught a class on the modern arts, and who read early versions of this book. Helen Wurdemann, at whose Art Association some of these chapters first appeared in lecture form.

Dick Hyland, agent and friend who handled talent and knew the West Coast jazz. Julia Johnson who showed me the jazz spots of the Middle West, and most of all the ones in South Bend. James Kern who sang in the early combos. Dudley Gordon of Los Angeles City College, who knows more about Americana than most. Lawrence Lariar, who in the twenties first introduced me to the music in New York.

Earle R. MacAusland, editor and publisher of *Gourmet* magazine for whom I went often to New Orleans to write of, among other things, the early jazz history, some of which first appeared in his pages. Jack and Francis Case, whose "Cavalcade of Records" on television was always able to answer a hard question, a record's history, and for their many kindnesses in aiding the author. Kenneth MacGowan of the University of California, where he teaches the art of the stage and its people. Ralph Rose for his knowledge and help with music. Joseph Schildkraut, not only a remarkable actor, but a man who remembers things about music and knows where to find them.

Jack Hellman and Dave Kaufman, both of *Variety,* bible of show business, who often helped sift the facts from the fiction. William Bacher, who explained many things from his early history in popular art forms. Jerry Wald, once a radio columnist, and with whom I tried to bring *Young Man with a Horn* to the screen.

Raymond Burr who has many rare records. James Gunn who knew all the places. Betty and Les Hansen of Magnolia Drive, who wore out a record player. John Wilson who spent months digging in old newspaper files for some very important items. Kerrin King, who at a time when this project needed help saw to it that the project made some money. Harry Longstreet, who with his camera copied out hundreds of old records and pictures and items, and printed them. Joan and Ethel, who live here and have to keep the files in order.

George Longstreet whose print collection has helped give historical detail. Jule Styne and Sammy Cahn, unashamed of Tin Pan Alley, with whom the author once ventured into musical comedy, with *High Button Shoes,* and learned what one form of popular music can be. Sidney Skolsky, producer, for whom the author wrote *The Jolson Story,* and Al Jolson himself, who wrote out for me the history of ragtime and showed how much real jazz differed from what he used as an entertainer. James Geller, himself a musical historian, who once interviewed Stephen Foster's last song-writing partner, and whose knowledge of classic and jazz music was much help. Maynard Stitt, now of Mobile, Alabama, who may do a book himself on the subject. Nell Boyd and Marian Dix Smith who kept track of the manuscript.

The Library of Congress for its books, files and recordings. Boris Godoff for his very large collection of early jazz sides. Poke Wilson who booked the early jazz bands and still has his ledgers of names and dates. The New York Public Library, the New Orleans Public Library, the University of Chicago Library. The files of the

New Orleans *Item,* the New York *Times,* the Chicago *Tribune,* the Los Angeles *Free Press.* Marty Klein for his collection of old jazz magazines and newspapers. Louis Epstein of Pickwick Bookshop. Lorser Feitelson for his memory of Le Jazz Hot in Paris in the twenties. The Huntington Library for certain details of Negro history. Eliot Paul for his boogie woogie piano playing.

And the jazzmen and women who are not named but who all helped.

STEPHEN LONGSTREET

September, 1956
Elm Drive
California

The Real Jazz Old and New

Oh, Basin Street is the street
Where black and white always meet
In New Orleans, land of dreams
You'll never know how sweet it seems
Or how much it really means . . .

OLD BASIN STREET BLUES

Chapter 1

In the Beginning

You can begin any place. The time they were dragging the black people out of the village clearings and moving them down to the coast, chained in long lines. You can begin when the stinking ships of the blackbirders crossed the bars below the delta and came up-river in flood, "the silt making the river a beginner's brown," and New Orleans idled in the sun behind its levees and old church-spires.

It's best to begin here, in New Orleans, where "the black man became in time a little lighter and the white men often a little darker." The French and the Spanish, the African tribesmen with royal chief's blood under their heavy muscles, and even the Indian peering in, the long boats from Kentucky, and the Yankee mountain men in buckskin fringes in for a big bust and swallowing of untaxed whisky, all wanted music and also made it.

"New Orleans mixed it all up and churned it around and was part of a south that was part of a new nation, that was part of a new world where anything can happen." Today we call it history. Simple people, wild people, pioneers and "men on their way up in a hurry, all sang a lot and stomped around to music." It came from the hills and from the polite music masters' minuets and string sections. But, best of all came out of black New Orleans, came first from the Negroes who had lost their birthright in that place. Here classic jazz began, and here it came to its full red-meat growth. New Orleans the way it was, and is, and even the way the tourists and the thrill-hounds see it. —Seaport, pleasure town, graveyard, slum, lake, country, bayou outposts; the reek and stink of it, the fun and dark laughter all mixed up, are just right for it. It had its Spanish and French troubles and the Civil War Yankees came and insulted the white women who spit on the Union flag. It had its dives, its sin and Mahogany Hall and its own kind of music.

The walls are dirty and unpainted and the brick-faced houses on Rampart Street and Canal Street divide the sheep from the goats, the hep ones from the squares. "Once they said it was all cypress swamp and mean dogs and lean squatters shaking with river fever. Then there was a man called Buddy Bolden, big and black and a scandal of a man. Drinking and cutting, he ran a barber shop and printed juicy stuff in a newspaper, and he organized a ragtime band. *Ragtime,* what the white folks called popular music, and which Buddy and his boys turned into something new, *jazzy,* JAZZ."

The old New Orleans places where they played are torn down now, flooded over, paved and made into fancy real estate. But there are other dives to move to and while the Eagle Saloon and the Masonic Hall are gone, their tunes aren't dead yet. "You hear them still, corner of Perdido and Rampart, and lonely at night on Bourbon Street, and in the shadows of the Church of St. Louis where the horse of General Jackson prances on his hind legs and the general sits, his hat off and held high cooling his copper brow, and beyond that is the river. The sidewalk place where the coffee and doughnuts are so good and the boys go there, bleary-eyed and shaky after a night of jamming and jazzing and reefer smoke, and tiger sweat called gin." The river has a green odor and the street is full of damp white sun.

You can talk about Storyville over the coffee—and the parties out on Lake Pontchartain and the fun on Fat Tuesday, called Mardi Gras. But mostly you talk about the slow hot blues and the old ragtime, loud and mean, and men and women who died young and left a dreadful body.

It's a good town for watermelon pink mouths and coffee and saffron-colored gals and tourist traps, the little bars where they come to look at the old colored men on the raised platform behind the bar still knocking it out on a horn, in memory of the plantation jazz. Towns too: Memphis and its Beale Street, and all along the Gulf Coast the little cigarbox banjos and tin-whistle bands make it music.

"The white professors wrote books about it so full of big words they right break your teeth, and the educated Creole niggers they wrote it out behind their bifocals and put their name on it, only it ain't rightly theirs. Some place in your head, the *bamboulas* are beating out the beat, and Congo Square is the place to be. . . . The dirty *wha-wha* tones of the good cornet is in the air." Even in Savannah, and in Chicago and on Central Avenue in Los Angeles, it's played now. But New Orleans was the pappy of it all. Shanty-town, Cajin, crapshootin' sport, Creole, big-footed mule driver, cotton hand and the big colored boys in the boxing rings . . . they all know it and like it.

It goes back to when the slaves first came, when the Louisiana Purchase wasn't just one for the history books, "or the birds." The dark folk came to the big weedy field at Orleans and Rampart, "to horse and act biggity and to laugh, to talk and find a boff. It was Indian country once (how we colored people get around), the real old ceremonial grounds of the Oumas Indians. But it became Congo Square. The white man calls it Beauregard, but Congo sounds better."

It was a place to try out the set of bones, the little tom-toms. The stuff that remembered Africa. Dancing and playing, shouting it out clear, *"Bamboula! Dansez! Bamboula! Badoum! Badoum! Bamboula!"*

Maybe it was a little voodoo, and the French-speaking Negroes who wore shoes and played in the little French orchestras might say *"C'est le Congo!"* But, incantations or not, it was the beginning of jazz. "Bamboula was the name of the drum covered with cowhide, a drum made of a length of bamboo. And before the brass came, before the valve horns came, there was a jaw-bone of the lop-eared jackass, his loose teeth making a light rattle when you hit them in tempo."

There was always work between music—hard work and mean work. A black man had to work, and there was work on the high-stacked packets, the gingerbread river-boats. "You stoked the furnaces with a pitch-knot pine, you toted the bales, you cut hair, and waited on table, and lit the fat cheroots and ran with cold mint juleps and poured the amber Bourbon. *Yes suh* and *yah man,* and if they tipped, you pocketed it and got out of the way of the gentry and the quality. Even if you didn't like it, you brayed the ole nigger laugh, *Yah Yah Yah!* the whites liked to hear. But when you played together in a session on deck and the white folk came around to listen, then you had them in the hollow of your big pink palm. River music, black music. *Jazz!"*

"They hired you for the boat-band and you faked it until you got the stuff locked away in your skull, and then you improved it little by little."

The Congo dances ended, and the boys got together to organize. The whole Mississippi Delta seemed jumping with jazz music, from the city itself to the cypress forest and the palmetto thickets. It was thickest in the Nouvelle Orleans, the original part of the town, now called the Vieux Carre or the French Quarter. The Creoles of color were thickest there, mixed bloods who looked down on the pure blacks but had the sense of music in their blood. The *menages,* the *mesamours* of quadroon gals and French gentry called for music and laughter, and the black bands played at their parties and dances, a little freer than in solid white society.

There was music on the river from the rivermen too who came

in lumber rafts and arks, in buckhorns and keelboats and the white and gold packets, with fat pine smoke ("black as God") pouring out of their stacks. *The Sultana, Belle of the West,* the *Robert E. Lee,* the *Enterprise* . . . Quay and wharves were full of business, passengers and hard-working black backs. It all mixed up in music along Desire Street and Piety Street, and in Storyville where people went for a bit of fun.

The street bands ragged a tune by taking one note and putting in two or three in its place. Buddy Bolden made a song of ragtime out of the street cries:

Any rags
Any rags
Any rags
Ain't you got anything today?

The string bass and cymbals were knocked around like drums in Africa had been, the horns and the piccolo and tuba and alto horn voiced the polyphony like a Gold Coast chorus. It sounded fine, not out of pitch and barbarous the way some said. Everything got mixed up a bit, work songs like *Drop That Sack,* and spirituals like *When The Saints Go Marching In.* Even the white coon songs, *Jump Jim Crow, Ole Zip Coon* and *Hamfoot.* The circus and minstrel bands showed how to make a trombone slide. And Scott Joplin was busy making rags like *Maple Leaf Rag.* There was Mill's *Georgia Camp Meetin',* and cake-walks like *Whistlin' Rufus.*

"And if you had no money for horns you played on harmonica, flageolet, homemade guitar and kazoo. Every chance to make music was fun. Even in the graveyards: Cypress Grove and St. Joseph's and the Lafayette. The band would march out behind the meat-wagon, black plumes on the hearse horses, playing *Free as a Bird* or *Nearer My God to Thee,* and then on the way home, *He Rambled 'Round The Town 'Til The Butcher Cut Him Down.*

"Music sounded good in the open, at Spanish Fort and Milneburg on Lake Pontchartrain playing a classic stomp, *Milneburg Joys.*

Also at the picnic park of the New Basin Canal and that wide-open town (man, it was wild), Bucktown. Sundays you drifted uptown to Washington Park trailing your horn or toting your bass, up to Carrollton Avenue. Or they hired you to ride a wagon with your band and play loud to announce riverboat trips, fast horses, strong fighters in the ring. The bands marched twelve to eighteen strong. Four cornets were not too many, an alto horn, an E-flat cornet, an E-flat clarinet. Now for dancing, seven men were enough, and noisy at that. The cornet took the legato runs and the arpeggios and did the breaks, the trombone buttered into the slides, there was a fiddle to show you had once heard European stuff; drums, guitar and string-bass finished it off. The piano wasn't used much until 1900. You couldn't carry it around, or run with it when you had to leave in a hurry."

Storyville, the red-light section of a dozen square blocks, was named after an alderman in 1897. The music that came out of the cathouses on Iberville and Liberty and Franklin and Bienville is still remembered. So, in time, the boys organized the new music on Franklin Street.

"Buddy Bolden had his barbershop there, and the boys knocked it around in the back room. Buddy, he hit it on cornet, and he did it better and newer than anybody had yet done it before. There were dance dates—playing at Tin Type Hall, and playing under the pecans over at Gretna. And Buddy and his cornet and his drinking, laughing, women-chasing. When the band paraded and every man had a woman to carry his stuff, Buddy had three women—one to carry his cornet, one his coat and one his hat. And you bowed to Buddy because his newspaper *The Cricket* was full of stuff you usually whispered before dawn in a bedroom with the shades fixed so the early morning breeze would shake out the odors of the nightlife and night music and night likker."

It was 1893 and King Bolden was busy playing every place with the boys. Perseverance Hall on Villere Street, and Tin Type Hall on

Liberty. "It was good and low-down. Gamblers, razor-bucks, high yellow hustlers, riverboys in with a packet, and the pool-hall sports with the fat faces and shiny skins. The whites didn't bother you too much, the dicty, fancy people stayed away. The church colored said it was sinful music, and the spiritual Baptists singers stayed with the Golden Chariot stuff, but their feet tapped and their hips swayed if they didn't watch themselves when they heard it." *Don't Nobody Go Away,* the music said, and the spirituals became the blues. Everybody danced very close and Buddy pulled his fat lip away from his horn and he sang it out over the throbbing heat of the dance-floor:

Way down, way down low
So I can hear them whores
Drag their feet across the floor!

Then King Buddy put that horn back in his face, to his lip, and he blew a phrase and then he shouted again:

Oh, you bitches, shake your asses.
Funky butt funky butt
Take it away!

Jazz wasn't at all respectable, you couldn't claim that. But it had something solid and something sad, and it *was.* "The whites were coming around and nodding. Some of them were hep to it and they explained it to you, why it was new and why it was great.

"It was certainly a new way to treat the horns, the C-clarinet, the B-flat, and the old piston trombone. When you needed a mute a gal's hat would do, or a beer-bottle, a coconut-shell or a big fat hand. You had to admit it started in the cathouse neighborhoods on Customhouse Street, in Nancy Hanks' Saloon, in the Liberty Halls, and the professor who couldn't read a note at the piano playing away ragtime and jazz and—as someone said—'so dumb-looking he didn't know what they did upstairs'.

"Mardi Gras meant lighted street-parades and money for the marching bands. Starting at Calliope Street and Charles, and up Royal, Canal and Orleans. The carnival balls were good jobs and you had to play it a little oldfashioned and somewhat European. But you could take a little of the stuff in B-flat, alley fiddle, muted horn and a hot kid on the skins.

"There was a clarinet player named Picou with the Olympia Band who wrote some music for the new boys: *Snake Rag* and *Muskrat Ramble* and *Alligator Hop*. The drummer played a four-beat bass on his stuff, on snare-and-rim, and knocked on the traps to match the moan of the valve trombone. And one night the boy on the doghouse bass broke his bow and he slapped it from then on with his hand.

" 'The Original Creole Band' one outfit called themselves and they went away on tours and played every place that would have them. That's how it began to travel. Then Nick LaRocca organized an outfit called 'The Original Dixieland Jazz Band,' and painted it on his drum. That was later, too.

"But poor old King Bolden, what had happened to him? Well, some said it was the likker and some said it was the yellow gals (and he did plenty of damage to both). But mostly his friends said, it was just that the man was worn out playing the music so much, and doing some sideline work and have all them interests of his. He blew his top—went on a tear during a big street parade."

They locked him up in the East Louisiana State Hospital, the place for the common nuts, in 1907, when jazz was already in its classic period. "They didn't let him play his horn. Got a white coat and they made him a barber again. And there he stayed—while jazz grew and the recording companies put the Stone Age stuff of jazz on wax, while the blue singers went out, Ma Rainey and Bessie Smith, and Louie Armstrong lipped his horn, while the cheap stuff came in and the jazz rose and fell like the tide and Tin Pan Alley horned in and faked it (some of it pretty good, most of it bad), while a fat man, a white one, came out of Denver and said 'I'm Paul Whiteman, the King of Jazz,' and wore clean clothes and gave a long-hair concert in JAZZ. And an East Side boy named Gershwin had a piece of his played: *Rhapsody in Blue*. All the best people applauded and the critics printed pages of fancy stuff about it. All that time, King Bolden cut hair in the booby-hatch, and jazz grew rich and famous, and grew popular and they invented the juke-box and the radio. The professors said it was a great new art form. The modern cats like Bartok and Schoenberg and Stravinsky gave it the nod. By that time, it was 1931. That year King Buddy Bolden, who made it work, he died."

Maybe he didn't feel a thing there at the end, still barbering behind the walls. But he had made it, had constructed a folk-art, maybe more. He had taken some simple ingredients, brass and blue times and good fun and low caressing, and had blown out a blended atmosphere, skillfully contrived to make a man jump outside himself, a woman take on the illusions that never paid off too much, cynical and romantic even when it was all goofer dust. "Sure it was vulgarity, a gaiety half tears, half gin, but it was beautiful the way Buddy played it, and dangerous. Anyway it became a unique folk-art, and extraordinary durable (they've been trying to knock it off for three generations now). It was baffling when you heard it far off, its mysterious elements potent the way it crept under your hide."

You can't tag it too much, the thing is often outside the realm of physical reason. Its earthy depravity, the heavy-lidded seductive pull of it, is balanced by the true blue honesty of it. For it was made by highly conscious artists, for all their insolent mocking beat. It was done with infinite pain characteristic of true genius, "unless that word scares you applied to Buddy Bolden hidden away from the world a long time, still hearing maybe the runs and the beat, still wanting that horn. But there wasn't anything much anyone knew anymore about King Bolden. As we said, when they were putting jazz into tails and white tie, Buddy Bolden, he who first whacked it together as an art form, he died. . . ."

Catch me stealin' Baby
Don't you tell on me.
If you catch me stealin', Baby,
Don't you tell on me.
I'll be stealin' back
To my old-time used-to-be . . .
If I don't do no better, Baby
Look for your daddy home . . .

BABY, DON'T TELL ON ME

Chapter 2

Blue Roots

There are two ways of telling the jazz story. One is to talk of the people and the dates, the places and the time; the other is to dig into the beginnings and the problems of making music, and the theory of it. You can try, as here, to combine the two. To see it and feel it, and to try to understand the thing that is music, and how this other music came along and changed it.

"Man always liked music because it wasn't so lonely when he could hear himself, and when he was angry or excited he shouted. He liked to hear himself a lot and he got a kind of rhyme and rhythm into it, maybe even before he could talk with words. He first made music by hitting something, and later he invented the bow—even before the wheel—and when he twanged the bow-string, that made music he liked. So he could beat it out, and he could pluck it on a string-bow. But it wasn't much at first and didn't become much for a long time."

We don't have to dig too deep into the past, because all that has been told before. What is important is that the first makers of jazz were closer to the cave-boy beating and twanging than the polite people who brought over the old stuff from Europe.

The pure Negro music has changed a lot since the slaves brought it with them and diluted it here. But we can still study Negro art-form and their ideas on art by looking at their Congo carvings, some of which go back six-hundred years and tell us what pure early Negro culture may have been like. It influenced native life then and still does a bit today, but Africa is changing so fast that you can't trust today's art-forms or sounds; they are only an echo in many cases of the real thing.

In Nigeria the bronze scarified heads are molded in forms that suggest the simple grace of the early blues. Some of these forms are almost two-thousand years old, but most of this is lost by time and fire and termites and jungle-rot. They are the symbols, like their music, of their rites and beliefs and to call them—as some Christians do—the artifacts of a pagan people is to call other people's gods names. *Nobody Knows But Jesus,* as music, is the same kind of line and form as the Congo girl with scarifications carved on her living skin, or on the wooden figures of the Baluba that house the spirit of the dead. The Negro hasn't changed his ideas of the spirit and the godhead, he has merely grafted a new name to old ideas. The Bapenda dancers today jumping and stomping, in fiber dress and clay paint, are the Congo Square forms of New Orleans, and the ideas of the Senufo ivory carvings became the early jazz notes and chords.

Working with a hand adze on jungle wood, or on a blues with a battered horn, the mind and marrow of the Negro are trying for the same thing. A ritual purpose decorating in geometric patterns his ideas, hopes and fears. His desires and joys, his erotic and normal visions of a short hard life.

The Benin, Ife and Bushongo artists' work was based on a keen observation of life in forms close to Euclid (and music is often pure geometry). Their ideas are arranged into objects, each with a personal form of its own but part of a whole culture close to the early blues and the early jazz, and part of something felt honestly, not for money and for fame; not in its beginning and its early growth. Jazz is frozen

Negro form and symmetrical curving ideas that made the music, or put the roots into it, just as the wood and bronze shapes inspired men like Klee and Modigliani to turn the stuff into a stylized painting. In painting it may only have the widespread appreciation of a fancy cult—but in jazz, it belongs.

It is better to study this early carving as the beginning of jazz rather than the native tribal tunes that some have captured on wax. For the music has been warped and changed, debased and traveled, and become worn and tired in many cases. But the real early carvings are still as strong and honest as they were when made.

"Your average jazzman doesn't know what he's talking about when he goes back and talks about this racial memory, and it's better to leave it at that because jazz is not and never was just the African forms. They were good bones, but on them were hung a lot of things. You have to remember that the makers of jungle music or tribal statues worked closely inside the only permitted forms. They did great work inside the taboos of their spiritual native limits. Jazz, by some, is held to be best only close to this limited outlook. But it has been growing and changing so much that no racial and tribal drawstring can ever be put on jazz. It's good to remember this when the purists begin to holler, 'please don't let them change it.' Negro carving remained a good but narrow art because it was limited; jazz can be knocked off by its admirers if they, too, try and keep it that crumby-sounding thing—primitive."

There isn't much agreement on jazz and everybody interested in the matter has a theory. The lovers of the form take a part of its history they think is real and earnest, and call other schools of jazz phony, and sweet, and for the trade. But they all agree that jazz is American and that it's a kind of phenomenon. And that it's only been around a little over seventy-five years. Also that it's pretty revolutionary stuff and that technically it's going to do a lot (if it hasn't already) to what is sometimes called Western music, sometimes European music, and often just longhair.

After these few admitted facts the lovers of the authentic jazz break up into little special groups, and they all analyze and define and evaluate in their own way. "The purists call jazz Afro-American music, which does it no harm, but doesn't define it enough or fully for something that came alive and kicking over seventy-five years ago in New Orleans, on the bayous and the deltas, right after what some call the Civil War, but down there is talked of as The War Between the States. It was a fusion of all the Negro musical forms coming together and made up of work-songs and blues, of hymns and whorehouse ditties, of spirituals and jail-house chants, all now called jazz. It was then called nigger-music, which means it was African in many ways, in spirit, in beat and technique. American folk-music of the marching brass bands of the homecoming deflated soldiers was used, also the memory of French dances; the polite but lively quadrille, the waltz and the polka. And, across the Gulf there seeped in notes from the Caribbean and Spanish-American ideas of popular music. It's not hard to find all this in the thing that suddenly came alive after boiling and bubbling a long time, and taking actual form when Emancipation was new and the Negro felt baffled, and yet elated by the big new day coming."

He danced and chanted in his Congo Square, in New Orleans, making his frenzy and his hopes a musical form that was, and is, a creative synthesis of all he remembered or borrowed or felt in the tempo of his blood. "It wasn't jazz then, just nigger music and it's remained that, at least to many of the admirers of the form, something only a Negro can do best and do well and do pure. The whites, when they tried it at first, made it only the cork-faced minstrel tune, or the coon melody of the *yak yak* school of black-face in silk coats and top hats. The real prime stuff was still in the honky tonks, the cathouses, the little back-road churches, in the jails." And just creeping into the Negro street parades.

So it came, music freely improvised and, as "slave-masters didn't teach harmony" and the art of reading and putting down music, it was all in the head. From there it went to the lips and the fingers of the musicmaker. If he played it different and only echoed what he remembered, you had to accept it as a synthesis of African and European stuff, but predominantly Negro and fieldhand and city-slums in character and playing. The work songs, the plantation hoedowns and the alley cakewalks all came in. The spiritual feeling of an ignorant but deeply hurt people brought to a borrowed white god. It was all there.

You find it all first coming alive and collecting around 1870—the assimilation and the first fumbling of the new technical stuff—there in the farmlands, the cotton and tobacco fields, where they were already calling it the blues. "It was mostly voice, because beyond the banjo and a little drumming there just were not the tools to make it instrumental. But in the cities like New Orleans, in Memphis and all along the riverfronts, as cheap and battered brass was picked up at bargain rates, the European instruments were on black lips and being used the way their makers never intended. It was rich and ropey, it was complex and, certainly, to the white ears, unique." By 1890 (a little ahead of our chapter) it was classic. It was American Negro and a long way from the ritual chant and the first field blues. It was the high tide to many lovers of the form, pure jazz at its peak.

Jazz has been explained a lot. Too often. You can say it's the subdivision in the beat implying personal accents, a synthetic working-together of two or more instruments aiding the solo performer. Whatever it is (admitting the base of the Protestant hymn for the blues, the Morris dance refining the drumming, the minuet for the cakewalk; and if you permit the start of the slave trade in 1442, when the Portuguese, Antam Gonsalvez, brought ten Negroes to Lisbon to save their Catholic souls and wear out their pagan limbs), jazz exists on real roots. Brought here to the U.S.A. because a prime black man was once worth $1,100.00 on the block in New Orleans ("only $350.00 in Cuba —so the Negro should have been happy to increase his worth by a little sea-trip"), jazz was bound to happen when the slaves got their own drumming and singing mixed a bit with Italian, Dutch and English ballads and madrigals. The cotillions went down the hill to become jigs, and when the first organ got into a church in Port Royal, Virginia, in 1700, those tones weren't going to be ignored.

The mountain and hunting grounds sang it all out:

Blow your horn and call your dog
We'll go back to the woods
And catch a ground-hog.
Rang-tang fiddle-de-day.

The slaves liked the lilt and meaning of that (ground-hog was eatable) and he added a lot of it to his personal music.

Everybody is striving to buy
And cheating each other
I cannot tell why
And it's hard, hard times . . .

The Negro field-hand certainly was amusing in his public moments. He liked to please (or act as if he did) and the white men soon were blacking up and playing "comic coons." In 1795, a Gottlieb Graupner came to Charleston from Hanover, Germany, liked banjo music and got into blackface and called himself "The Gay Negro Boy" at Boston's Federal Street Theater. Another fake darkie was Thomas "Jim Crow" Rice, who, in the 1830's, hung around livery stables and got up, or invented:

Wheel about, turn about,
Do just so,
And every time I wheel about
I jump Jim Crow.

With the end-men and the walk-around, the white minstrels were on their way, and the very ritual procedure was to remain unchanged, like a mass, until today. To say all of this didn't help real jazz when it came along would be nonsense. By 1871 the Negro Fisk Jubilee Singers were touring, and so true Negroes on the stage were accepted enough to make well known *Deep River, Go Down Moses, Swing Low Sweet Chariot* and *Little David, Play on Your Harp.* From these came the first true blues.

The dilution of the pure African music had to come. The best example of the early stuff is the Afro-American spiritual that brought the Congo, and God, into the strawpen together. The good archaic blues, the early classics, are history now, and to call them "the only pure jazz" is the fantasy of a minority. Deformation of Negro jazz had to come, and so did the periods of decadence within jazz itself. It happened in modern painting when Negro carving hit the school of Paris just after the turn of the century, and what was Negro and what was classical painting of Europe never came out pure anymore, but it certainly came out as an exciting new way to look at a wall.

Every era or art, the historians say, has a beginning, a middle and an end: a language, a race, a culture, and even a universe. So jazz has a beginning and it begins in Africa and most of it begins on the West Coast of Africa. The slavers imported an art-form that was primitive and satisfying, and it was mixed here with the poor white ballads of the Scotch and the remains of the mountain Elizabethans, the white river melodies of the keel-boat men and the wagon trains.

The Negro never heard the white stuff right or pure and he translated it all into his own message, so that the hymn did duty soon as the spiritual, and, after a long while, transformed again by erotic overtones, it became the blues, and was so new it owed very little to its grandpappy, the hymn. Back on the African coast, the native music was centuries old, with a rhythm and tone as ritual as the proper way to bow to the Queen of England. Like all music it started as shouting and became dancing, and the two merged to become song. The black people danced and sang because they were frightened at the cruel evil in the jungle, at the storms and animals and the witch-doctors' gestures. And they danced and sang because they liked the beat and the things it did in many strange ways to their emotional feeling and their mating habits.

They did it because there wasn't much else to do in village clearings, when the moon was right and they wanted to express something of what they felt about life and their ideas of things that made the thunder and the fat hips of the girls. They also wanted to tell of hunting and Arab slave-raiders and all the stuff that is life. They made poems out of it and dotted it with drums and reed fifes. Their music was a highly developed art, as high in the scale as the wood-sculpture they did along the Congo, at Gabon, and the delicate and advanced bronze pouring at Benin. Just as jazz was to change music, so these wooden and bronze forms were to change modern art.

Drumming and tribal singing were more than fun and fear—they were the religious life, the social life, the education, the Yales and Harvards of the jungles. Harmony as we know it is there in the chanting consecutive thirds, fourths and fifths; they rise and they come down. It's a device that sounds beautiful and helps the melodic line and doesn't get in the way of the rhythm. Their chain chords were to come over to the blue spirituals almost untouched. The Negro range is wide: from the ceiling falsetto to the gravel voice and the reed flutes and the drum-beats trying to match it. It was singing merged to percussion rhythm, and the drum did a good job in many sizes, with hands or sticks as motor-power.

It wasn't all alike, but it was related and the slaves from Dahomey, Yoruba and Ashanti came to America almost before the *Mayflower* to become early settlers. Sometimes they stopped on the way at Haiti for a generation or so, and the voodoo came along to make it just a little bit more solidly native. New Orleans saw a lot of these tribes.

They brought along their percussion; the drums, the hand-claps, feet-stomping or shuffling along. The drums had a cross-rhythm the hands and feet picked up. When the slave-owners broke the drums for turning the slaves to tiring pleasures, they built them in secret and you can find an actual drum from Virginia dated 1728. The prints show Negroes drumming in Congo Square, in New Orleans, around 1817.

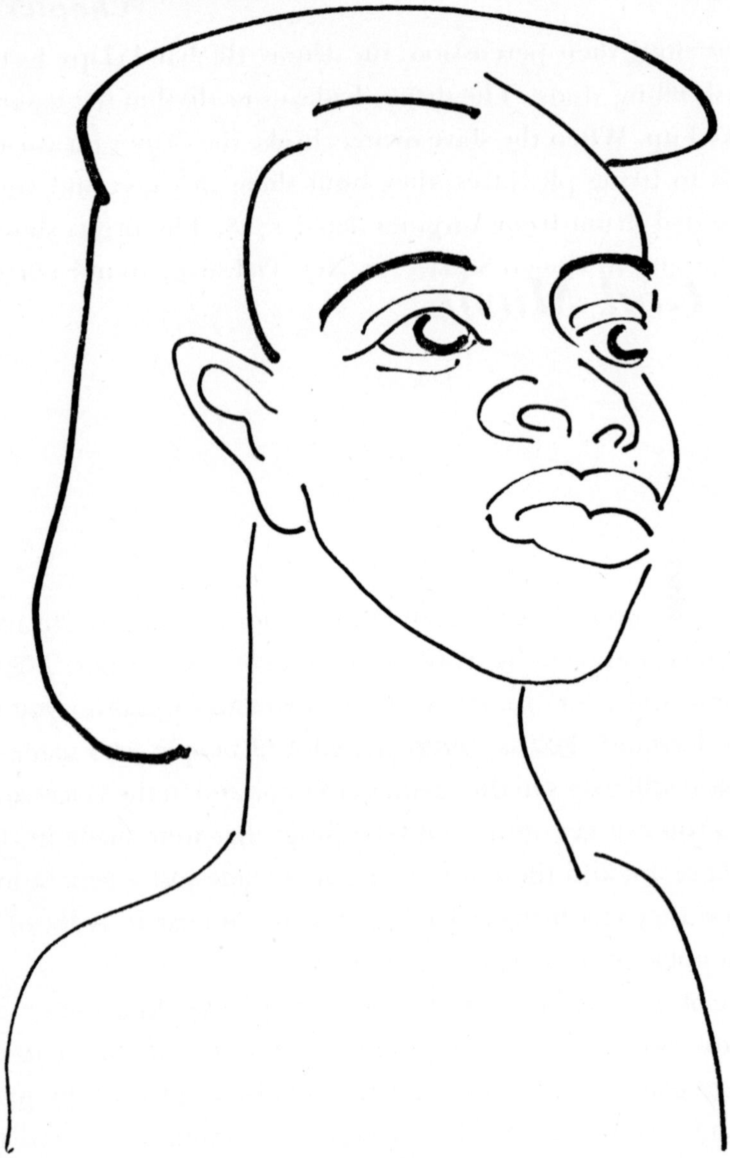

Hand it pretty poppa, mama wants some lovin' I found
Hand it pretty poppa, momma wants some lovin' right now
When I was nothin' but a child
When I was nothin' but a child
All you men tried to drive me wild . . .

RECKLESS BLUES

Chapter 3

Black God Music

If you want to study most art-forms you have to live in the museums, and take the word of the writers of old books. There is a lot of time and a lot of history between you and whatever you're trying to understand. Jazz is different. A lot of people who made it are dead, but it still exists in the memory of some and in the voices and horn-sounds you can get out of old recordings that were made in the old way. There are also thousands of records made just a generation or so ago and they can bring it back, and you can hear it. A lot of it was bad, but not as much as you would think.

Some of it is hard to find. The junk-shops, the old-clothes men no longer are foolish about it; they know the worth of the platters. But there are places where you can *hear* the history of jazz, the just-gone past, and it will give you a better idea of what went into jazz than any book like this.

You can trace it from Africa, you can see the beginning and the coming-together of the thing called jazz. To hear it right you have to understand what to listen for, what stayed and what went. The Negro made his wood carvings and his bronze casting art, yet remained within the limits of the fetish, the ritual of his art. Jazz also began within certain strict forms.

The old percussive polyrhythm was mostly a continuous repeated round called an *ostinato*. When the drum joined the first bands, it kept its job of keeping the beat. The lead cornet was the bandleader and set the tempo and knocked out the lead phrases. The voices were replaced by the trombone and clarinet, being melodic where the voices had been choral. The boys added free improvisation of rhythmic variation, a kind of mutation carried as far as endurance and wind and lip could take it. Also one rhythm could ride piggy-back on another rhythm superimposed by the horn section concurring in syncopated phrases.

When they got around to affording a piano and moving indoors, the left hand took over the rhythm with not much improvisation and the right hand made improvised music. That had once been the job of the drums and voices. A horn in jazz is anything in brass; cornet, trumpet or saxophone. The clarinet, of wood, is also a horn. The trumpet has a tendency to make, with the multiple repeating of the same note, a single note held a long time—broken pedal point as it's called. It goes back to Africa with or without rhythm variations.

All music has a language and started as language, and jazz inherited from the African tongues the thing the language is—tonal. Its vocabularies were built up on many changes in the vowel sounds. The Chinese are pretty vowel, and it comes out in their music, too. So jazz is a vowel kind of music. Africans and American-Africans had a music before jazz and it was all vocal, made up of voice instruments and then played that way when they got horns and a piano.

The source was always fresh. Captain John Smith brought in "twenty negars" to Jamestown in 1619, and the last slave was shipped over in 1864, so refresher-courses from the music colleges in the jungle went on for a long time. The slaves sang because this was almost the only form of expression open to them. It gave the slave rhythm for his muscles and gave his mind a job: singing. Their work-songs helped lift the bale and tote the barge. Nobody paid too much attention to

Negro music for a long time. Thomas Jefferson wrote: "In music, the Negroes are more . . . gifted than the whites. . . . The instrument proper to them is the *banjar.*" The work-songs are still sung in the chain-gangs, the farm jails of Texas, Louisiana and Mississippi. "The work-holler and chant keeps time with the clink of chain, the bark of prison hound-dogs, the buzz of night-insects in the road-camp when the blues fit a man's lonely mood. The work-holler, the river-holler and the fisherman-holler are all different. And the cornfield-holler called *Arwhollie* is still heard, as *Don't Mind De Weather.* Full of long, sliding tones, you find hollers in many of Lead Belly's recordings and songs." Huddie Ledbetter, as he was known in his more formal moments and on police-lists, was "The King of the Twelve-String Guitar." He was a ghost from the past, the last of the real holler-song singers.

Drumming and dancing were frowned upon by the slave-owner as wearing out the working strength of the slaves. He gave them instead something he had that didn't cost anything—his religion. The Negroes took from it what they needed, or understood, and added a little of the mumbo-jumbo and flare from their own heritage. But secretly they still made drums and danced when they could. *Juba,* one of the earliest dances, is supposed to be the authentic stuff from Africa. *Green Corn* and *Corn-Bread Rough* also were farm dances. So music, religious and erotic and secular, grew up shoulder to shoulder. The erotic and secular were called by the church folk sinful and worldly, but many partook of both.

"When the slave came to talk to God with a banjo he played what he heard by ear, or liked by ear. And when he got a piano he played it sinful or godlike. He played his music in clapboard churches, or for the purpose of the open-air evangelist, or he became the professor in a Storyville whorehouse, with ragtime or barrelhouse, in saloons or wherever music was wanted for a burial or a parade or a fish-fry." With no writing to put it down, the same music had many versions. *Swing Low Sweet Chariot* is a different song in its different versions. The church music had great feeling. In *On That Great Gittin'-Up Mornin'* and *I Hope My Mother Will Be There,* the lament of the Negroes reaches a high level of folk-art.

"The Negro sang when he cut cotton or hoed 'tater-plants, carried water, chopped sugarcane, tied leaf-tobacco. He sang on the levee and on the railroad, shouted in holy trance, hollered in the streets selling soft-shell crabs and York cabbage. He made it a square dance and a cake-walk, jig and ragtime stomps and struts and even the small-fry sang their hiding songs and ring songs and street-corner rhymes." There were ballads of sad fates and hard blows, and even epics about *John Henry,* who loved like a bull stallion and worked like a steamboat engine racing a packet to St. Louis. "There were gambling songs and songs of women and whores, about yellow girls and lovin' and fightin' and razor-brawls in smoky dives and spangles on honky-tonk flesh. Smoke and whisky and tumbled bodies all came into the music. It was low-down and mean, and it was beautiful and earnest toward God. It was everything inside the world of the black man that meant meat, work, love and trouble." From the *Jelly Roll Blues* to *I'm Goin' To Lift My Standard for My King,* the music ran the gamut "from sweet children's voices respecting the pore Christ-chile, to the dirty tone blues about a man, a good man, and a bad woman in a bed."

The intellectual today likes to listen to the *Circumcision Ritual of the Babira,* and he will accept *Run Ole Jeremiah,* but he will often frown on the plain low-down wail of Bessie Smith. He likes:

I got a rock
You got a rock
Rock is death
Oh, my Lord,
Run here Jeremiah
I must go on my way
Who's that riding the chariot?

This is deep and respectful. But a song like *Put It Right Here and Keep It There* is also close to the problems of this world:

I've had a man for fifteen years,
Give him his room and board.
Once he was like a Cadillac—
Now he's a worn-out Ford.

The Negro was never the material realist and his songs had the fine true feeling of the accepting of magic. *Ain't No Grave Can Hold My Body Down* and *Jesus Make Up My Dying Bed* show him treating his God with respect, but as a mutual partner in misery.

People with no written history sing their epics, and the Negro sang ballads. But the whites of the south sang them too, and the two got mixed up at times, so that the music of the slave-pens and the scabby-hill acres of the descendants of Scotch bondboys crossed that of the so-called Cavaliers ("Dukes don't emigrate"). Ballads were the newspapers, the gossip-columnists, the social documents and the breezy exchange of events among the unread.

The white men with their own banjos and jugs and cigar-box fiddle-music did a lot to inject something into jazz. The snobbery of some later critics have made jazz all Negro, and mostly it is, but the hill-whites and the fever-shaking crackers and the rivermen in their shanty-boats produced *Barbara Allen* and *Froggie Went A-Courtin'* and *Casey Jones.*

When the Negro, using the white ballads as models, tried his own, he got *Frankie and Albert* which led to the more famous *Frankie and Johnny, Lily and Frankie Baker.* Also *Ole Master Had A Yalla Gal* and *Mr. Boll Weevil.*

Frankie and Albert had a lot of grandchildren. A dozen later songs are suggested by some of its lines:

Rubber-tired carriage
Kansas City hack
Took poor Albert to the cemetery
And forgot to bring 'im back.

Oh, he was my man,
But he done me wrong!

The Negro kids picked up the mood early—that music helped one along in life. They sang as they played hide-and-seek:

All hid?
All hid,
Five ten fifteen twenty
Is all hid?

Way down yonder
By the devil's town
Devil knocked my daddy down
Is all hid?

It was the church laments that were to lead to the blues that had the most feeling and tenderness:

I wonder as I wander out under the sky
How Jesus, our Saviour, did come for to die
For poor orn'ry people like you and like I
I wonder as I wander out under the sky.

Someone has divided these songs as the songs of the whites and the songs of the blacks. But no one really knows who sang them first and a lot of them were sung by anyone who felt God in the strawpen when he came forward to ask for his sins to be washed out, or dipped under, or laid away with hands:

You got to cross that lonesome valley
You got to cross hit by yourself,
There hain't no one goin' to cross hit for you
You got to cross hit by yourself.

Death was real to them, and mean and cruel, and they knew the true meaning, free of ritual and incense and Latin when they sang:

Dey pierced Him in the side
De blood came a-twinklin' down,
An' he never said a mumblin' word.

Wasn't it a pity and a shame?
Dey nailed Him to the tree
An' he never said a mumblin' word.

He bowed His head and died.
Wasn't it a pity and a shame?
An' he never said a mumblin' word.

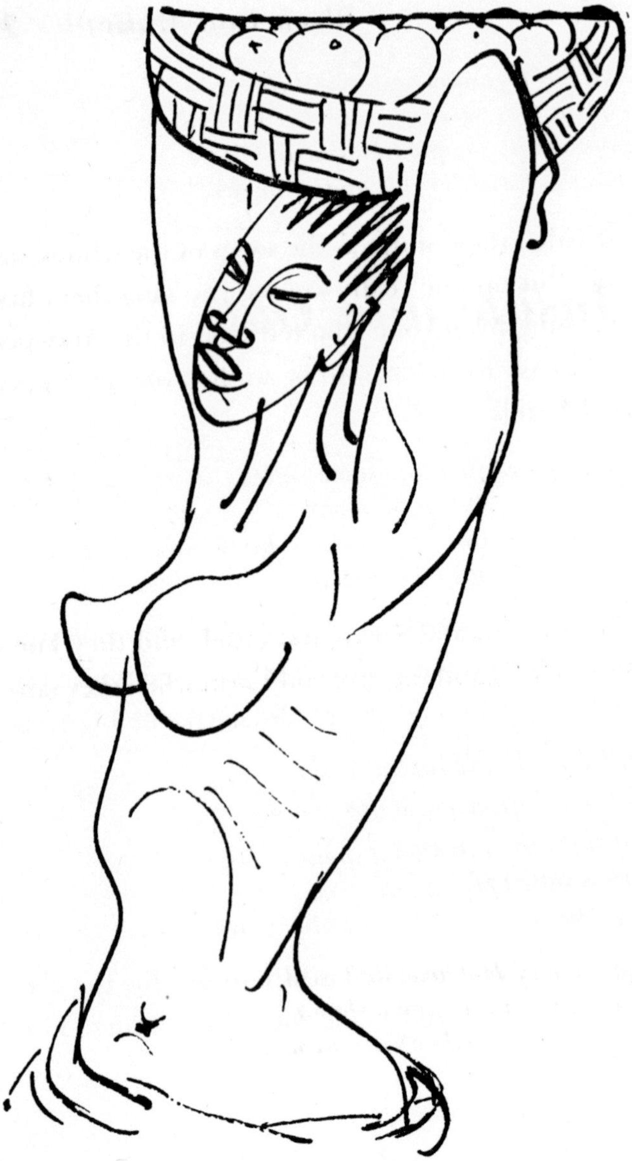

All de doctors you kin try
All de medicine you kin buy
Yet you gotta lay down
Someday an' die . . .
FIELDHAND BLUES

Chapter 4

The Music Inside and Out

The real music came from deep inside and made you—the singer—feel good when you got it out. But you used music for many things. In the markets you could laugh and carry the big load and shout out what you had to sell:

Veg-etub-bles! Guinea squash!
Tomat-tuhs! Sibby beans!
Hard-head cabbage!
York cabbage!

Or along the waterfront; carry and peddle and shout out for the seafood that wasn't too hard to catch, and made such good eating. The best voice sold the most:

Oystyuhs! She-crab!
Raw shrimp!
Raw! Raw!
Raw!

"But when it came to the blues, then something else entered into it, and the voice and the music of street-cries became something different, something you couldn't always understand, but that in the end was the deep-felt things, the things you laughed and horsed around to forget. You couldn't just climb up to it, directly.

My God is so high you can't get over Him,
He's so low you can't get under Him.
He's so wide you can't get around Him,
You must come in by and through the Lamb.

The white man gave you that, the blood of the Lamb, but what you did with it was something else. . . ."

To the maker of early jazz, it was more than just blowing certain notes in certain remembered ways, more than changing and improvising as he went along. Often he was trying for much more, but he couldn't have put it into words. In a way his music was trying to attain to the level of a moral symbol, for himself and for humanity. Maybe he did it in the genres of caricature at first, but that was only a surface reading, because the Negro mind, even in reality, has the intensity of fantasy and symbolism. Music, jazz, is after all an abstract art, and so the results the player got were abstract, but based on the world as he knew it, suffered and dreamed it could be. With him it assumed often a delicacy and a grotesque poetry that throws off the imitation of nature and takes on in his best work a free creative effort. His work, like all true art, makes us laugh or cry, and when he is a genius it can give us ecstasy.

Jazz is certainly a unique business; it can introduce us to the sublime when its feet are still tapping out a boogie-beat. It becomes the enormity of the real without leaving the reek and smoke of the barrel joints. The totality of feeling that comes out of a brass horn is amazing in its discordant elements. Maybe it's because jazz carried no burden of long words, cultures, or intellectuals' concerts in the playing; so that, like the primitive ignorant saint in ecstasy, it is an emotion in many cases beyond taking apart and examining. The music intuitively grasps the heroic loneliness of a people. It is the art of withdrawing, retiring into oneself, yet moving on to the glory of its musical form. From mammy-jamming to concert jazz, no matter how sleek, some tinge of this appears. Satchmo has just to put his horn to his scarred lip for us to realize a synthesis of blue light and blue shade. The scheme of this simple colorist blows apart, for a moment, anyway, the absurdity of prejudices. Jazz—when it works—has a sad gravity between the dirty-toned *wha wha* and the jackass growls, a robust and effective bitterness against cruelty, against the academic precision of the past in music. The style is never obtained by any concession to prevalent taste.

Only the significant objects of life share in expressing the jazz mind blowing through a horn. The jazzman draws his music directly from nature and material objects, but he draws them out of their corny anonymity, making them share and take part in the dream and reality of the world. The very piano comes alive and snarls in ironic rage. The Negro, however, is never, in Baudelaire's words, "genius sick with genius." He inspires serenity when he gets down in earnest to his blues. His work becomes a spontaneous negation of the pork-chop, fried chicken, watermelon minstrel-show myth in burnt cork. His certainty is real when he blows the music to his limited knowledge of his moral values. He may never suspect any artistic image, any new musical or spiritual values. But jazz does—at its early best—keep the folk sanity, the ease of impulse that makes jazz just about the only true native art. Big or small, it is not our place just yet to decide. Going from a freebee to Carnegie Hall, the journey up for jazz is not over, and not yet fully charted. "Lots of folk still can't see for lookin' how groovy a simple thing can become. And how it can brown-off when the money and easy times come in. . . ."

The blues added up everything that is jazz in one complete and complex bundle that became jazz folk-art. They took a long time growing but when they were ready, the blues were exciting and something the world saw for its worth as a spontaneous, yet creative, effort of a people. The black man looking for a spiritual horn of grace, accepting the flesh when he couldn't get the spirit, and being let down to loneliness, made a profound—yet simple—thing of life, the nucleus for what was going to be New Orleans jazz.

It was never the music of nice comfortable well-bred people. It was the hungry notes of the disinherited, the enslaved and the ignorant. "It was the drink-filled meanness of a red-eyed nigger with a knife, it was the chained man in a lousy cell, it was the cheap gab of a diseased whore, it was cold and rainy and it was steamboat steam and rivers in flood and mud every place. It was slavery and yellow girls in the planter's bed, and the breeding-pen for the slave markets. Sometimes it was the cake-walk and the breath of animal odors of the circus; it was brassy parades marching to bury a lodge-brother with a ragtime dirge, *Didn't He Ramble*." It had the surface of true art; simplicity, earnestness and starkness.

"Blue music is antiphonal: singing a melody in antiphonal phrases while the instrumental polophony is busy as a fiddler's elbow weaving the music. The trumpet takes to the tremolo which shakes hell out of the timbre and tampers with the pitch. You can play it open or with a mute of corn-cob, hat or hand—and it goes from the real high notes to a deep growl, getting dirty as it takes on the low-down tonal variations. The notes count and the two that are the real blue ones are the flatted seventh and third. An extended blue scale is something to hear."

By 1870 the blues were ready and hot and in the form we know them today. As a rule, blues are almost always a song-form, usually a solo. The shouting blues are based on the hell-fire preaching styles of the colored churches, but used for sinful music. The melodic blues are lower in key and give the melody a break. The dramatic blues recite and the lyrics are sweet. But mostly the best blues combine a little of each.

"The blues took hold hard in the cities where life was tough, living a struggle, and sin a next-door neighbor. They moved from

New Orleans to Birmingham; went to St. Louis, to Memphis by slow freight or by Steamboat Gothic. Kansas City and Chicago soon knew them." Later there were famous names, at least to the lovers of the form—Louie Armstrong and the voices of Ma Rainey, Bertha Chippie Hill, Maggie Jones, Bessie Smith, Billie Holiday, Sippie Wallace, Hociel Thomas. From 1920 to 1930 a lot of these made wax recordings, but they started long before that. Ma Rainey was belting out the blues in 1901, and around 1907, at twelve, Bessie Smith was doing the same.

Again some say "the classic blue period is gone to hell in a hack and only in some church can you find it pure and good." But the classic becomes, in time, fit only for the museum, and the blues are still growing—debased often, faked a lot in Tin Pan Alley, but progressing according to some, finished as anything but popular music according to others.

A deep contralto and a good blues number are still worth hearing. Today Lonnie Johnson, Roosevelt Sykes and others carry on the form. The claim that blues were vulgarized into pornography is often made by the serious critic of pure jazz. But these critics lack humor. The blues were fully erotic when they began and will always bear their share of the troubles of sexual partners and two-timing women and men. When the blues are truly decadent and sophisticated, they are usually written for the cafe society market and the smart advance guard groups that see only the smut in the stuff. Obscenity can often be the spice of wit and music, and the basic problem of life is that faced by a man and woman in passion.

To reject modern blues because some are fashionable and slick is to curtail the writing of the music. There are only good songs and bad songs. Some music is always better than other music, even in the same form. T. S. Eliot will never have the lusty Elizabethan fury of Shakespeare, and Keats never descends to the popular riming of Kipling—yet all wrote "verse-form." So the blues-singers and their material are not all equal. The slick chicks who play to the smut-hounds only have produced a pretty good blues called electric, but it doesn't hold its own with the gutty stuff of Lead Belly singing *Cat Man Blues*

Cat man cat man
Stay away from my door
At night.
Prowlin' round my back door
When I'm gone
You know that ain't right.

or *The Blind Lemon Blues* or *The Raidin'-Squad Blues.*

Jimmy Yancey as much as anyone created the boogie-woogie blues, and his followers—Meade Lux Lewis, Pine Top Smith, Albert Ammons and others—carried on the job.

Make me a pallet on the floor
Make me a pallet, Baby,
A pallet on your floor
So when your good gal comes
She will never know.

Make it soft and low
Make it Baby soft and low
If you feel like layin' down, Baby
With me on the floor
When your good gal comes home
She will never know.

I ain't no high yeller, I'm a beginner brown
I ain't gonna marry, ain't goin' to settle down.
I'm gonna drink good moonshine and run these browns down
See that long lonesome road, Lord, you know it's gotta end . . .

YOUNG WOMAN BLUES

Chapter 5

Blues Singing Gals

They didn't sing the blues in the rich places, in the smart nightclubs in the old days. They went on tour, played black-and-tan joints, the smoky little places, the broken-down roadhouses, the ratty vaudeville houses failing to fight off the movies. It was a time and an era before people knew the blues were art, and it was a hard livin' and a lonely thing.

"It was best heard late at night when the lights were so low you couldn't see the peeling paint, and the scars on the waiters, and the plumbing had settled down to gurgle. The front tables were pretty well filled and the joint smelled of booze and face powder and happy sweat. The band wasn't tired any more, and the drum-skins were shiny and the piano player was beginning to bend lower over the eighty-eight keys of the ivory floor. Then in the yellow mist of a spotlight and smoke would come this black gal in purple face powder. Maybe no longer so young, big in the butt and carrying a proud stomach and a set of knockers in a dress dry-cleaned too often. After the introduction, she opened her mouth and if she had gold in her dentistry, it showed. Once she started singing the blues, nothing mattered—smoke, cold, cheap likker, the rent-money or the job. There wasn't anything like a good blues singer singing the classic music, making the old favorites stand at attention. It wasn't always sung the way you heard it before. But if it was Ma or Bessie, nobody could do it better."

Way down in Boogie Alley
Ain't nothin' but skulls and bones
An' when I get drunk
Blues goin' to take me home.

The real blues are deeply felt. *Dyin' Rider Blues, Hell Hound on My Tail,* are near to the dirty business of death seen with a directness that is close to much fancy poetry.

The first masters of the blues, the singers, were powerful gals. Gertrude Ma Rainey is said by many to have been the best and, certainly, the first great one. She was born in Columbus in Georgia, and the date is supposed to be April 26, 1886. Her folks were Negro minstrel people who trouped the country. When only fifteen, she married Will Pa Rainey, and went out with him in the Rabbit Foot Minstrels, already singing the blues. She sang the blues in rain or shine, in tent-shows and low-down joints, in camps and on the stage. The Theatre Owners Booking Association—a Negro vaudeville circuit—took her on and she grew famous and sometimes she got a little money together. "Ma was short and she was heavy, and she was real black. Ma found a kid named Bessie Smith in Tennessee, and helped her up."

Ma invested her money in theaters in Rome, Georgia. For almost forty years she sang the blues. Her recordings are primitive things and only hint at the greatness of her putting over a blues number. About fifty of her recordings—a hundred sides of her songs—are on records. They were mostly made for the Negro trade on the obsolete acoustic process, sung into a horn with no microphone or electrical engineering. She sang it somber and simple, she sang it mellow, her vibrato easy and broad. Ma took the rocking rhythm and made it monumental. Her best stuff is found in *Levee Camp Moan, Moon-*

shine Blue, Shave 'em Dry, Slow-Drivin' Moon, Jelly Bean Blues and *See See Rider.*

Her basic background instrumentation is the horns, piano, drums and banjo. Louie Armstrong did some of his best early work for her. He was still influenced by King Oliver, and Bunk Johnson. The trombone was often in the hands of the now-forgotten Charlie Long Green, who later froze to death in a doorway (a not unusual fate for the early jazz player).

See See Rider
See what you done done
Lawd, Lawd, Lawd
You made me love you
Now your gal's done come.

I'm gonna buy me a pistol
Just as long as I'm tall
Lawd, Lawd, Lawd
Gonna kill my man
And catch the Cannon Ball
If he don't have me
He won't have no gal at all.

Ma Rainey retired, and died, at the age of fifty-three on December 22, 1939.

"Then there was Bessie Smith, who toured the South a long time and sang a lot of blues. She didn't save her money and she didn't worry too much about what she sang. But she sang it deep and well. She made big money when the best of the jazz-players still carried their horns in paper bags and didn't know where their next bottle of gin was coming from. She hit a thousand dollars a week playing for colored groups in the Negro cities.

"She made a lot of smoky stuff on records that some people don't like. But it was in her style and in her mood and even when it was pretty vulgar, she very often made it sound better than it was. She even sang the fake coon songs of Tin Pan Alley. She was big, and she was solid bronze, and Bessie took hold of it with two big hands and when she faced the customers, she made the blues have the meaning that was all her own." Bessie left almost two-hundred issued sides of recordings.—She did *Jazzbow Brown, Careless Love, Put It Right Here, Spider Man Blues, Empty Bed Blues, Hard Drivin' Papa* and *Black Water Blues.*

Love O Love O careless love
You flood into my head like wine,
You wrecked the life of many a poor gal
An' you left me with this life of mine.

Night and day I weep and moan
You brought the wrong man into this life of mine
For my sin till Judgment I will atone.

Nobody has yet written a great big blues on the death of Bessie Smith. It could be a fine one; the *Auto Death Blues.* Bessie died as the result of an auto accident in 1937 at Clarksdale, Mississippi. Taken with some injured white people to a hospital, she bled to death of neglect while the whites were treated first.

Ma and Bessie sang it the way they felt. Ferdinand Jelly Roll Morton took the old solid blues and he sang them, often transformed in his own ways. He gave them a lyric polish, an almost French elegance. He added a lot from ragtime, and he pushed a little further the horizon of harmonic and melodic ideas. He was no easy man to get along with. He knew he was good and his bump of ego was salted with genius. He was a creative jazz man, not just a performer; part naive, part mean. Jelly Roll was the artist living inside himself and getting lyric stuff from the distilling of his love of the jazz form. His piano accompaniment was the easy merging line of voice and piano doing a good job. His best were *Winnin' Boy, I Thought I Heard Buddy Bolden Say, Doctor Jazz,* and *Michigan Water Blues.*

Hociel Thomas was not the powerhouse of the early blues singers. She stuck pretty close to the churchlike blues and she made music plain, on the beat. She did a lot of spoken words to a horn's obbligato, and Louie Armstrong worked with her a lot (he seems to have worked with everybody a lot). When she did her *Gambler's Dream,* she was doing the best she could do—and her best was classic.

"Some came and went fast, didn't last, just did a few things that stayed." Bertha Chippie Hill had a deep voice, the power and then some. A handful of Okeh records remain to show what she had. She dropped out of sight and then, in 1946, she did some recordings and they still had the old punch. *How Long Blues* and *Trouble In Mind.*

Trouble in love comes with me
An' it sure does grieve my mind.
Some days I feel like livin'
Sometimes I feel like dyin'.

I'm goin' lay my head
On some lonesome railroad iron
An' let the 2:19 train
Satisfy my mind.

Sippie Wallace had a shouting quality full of the quavering phrases. She was best in *Trouble Everywhere I Roam, There's No Hidin' Place* and *Baby I Can't Use You No More, Section-Hand Blues* and *Parlor Social Deluxe.*

Down at that renthouse party
Each and everybody
Git full of gin and corn
An', folks, they had their habits on
Big business for some bootlegger
An' bigger business for the undertaker.

"Later, the blues were still sung and written and some good people were involved. But, as in everything, the cult for the old has taken over in jazz. So a lot of the new blues are supposed to have a falling-off in power. This may be, but it's too soon to judge and history has the habit of making today's fresh songs into tomorrow's old classics." Roosevelt Sykes, Lonnie Johnson, Jazz Gillum, Lil Green and Josh White carry on with blues singing. *Deep Water Blues, Fine and Mellow, When You Feel Low-Down, Milk Cow Blues* have all been called cliché, sophisticated and, often, pornographic. Somehow each generation's critics seem shocked to find sex still doing business.

Progress, even in a new form like jazz, is rejected by many of its most ardent followers. All popular music has a fringe that becomes artifice and insincere, but all the true poignant melancholy of the blues would blow away if each new generation—black or white—didn't try its version of the thing. While jazz is Negro—born and raised—it should be for everybody who wants to listen, and wants to play.

Supply did not keep up with demand of the real home-baked stuff, and the pseudoblues came into being. But to call all Harlem jazz phony is unfair. "They took what came north and fitted it to the needs of their crowded streets, their rent parties and reefer joints, their dance halls and their creep dives, their muggers and crapmen and swing-dancers, their city ways and fancy padded clothes. Maybe *Wang Wang Blues, Mobile Blues* and *Washdog Blues* aren't in true Southern accents, but they served the purpose for which they were written."

The purists have also gone after the hide of W. C. Handy, "Father of the Blues." To insult him, he's called an offshoot of the Fisk Jubilee Singers. A pioneer is often condemned for not killing all the Indians in the woods, instead of just clearing enough timber to make a clearing to live in. But within his limits, Handy has done a good job. He wrote it down, and that was one reason he's not liked by some. He took what he heard and what might have been lost and forgotten and made it real and solid, like *Yellow Dog Blues* and *St. Louis Blues.* Poets, novelists and painters dislike their own contemporaries, as anyone knows who has sat in with them talking shop. So makers of jazz will set up a few gods like Pops Armstrong and Bunk Johnson and Jelly Roll Morton, and get out the knife for almost everyone else active in the jazz world. This is too bad, but it's human nature, and so the sight of the usual dogfight among the followers of the blues inside jazz is not to be taken too seriously. The good will stay, the bad will be forgotten.

The big talk against writing it down is that jazz is not composed music, but improvised in performance. Therefore anyone who writes it down is out of the true jazz tradition. Which is like saying only blue-eyed men are members of the human race, brown-eyed men are only trying to be like blue-eyed men. There is room in jazz for the written, and the improvised. You don't improvise from nothing. You take a phrase that exists in mind, or on paper, and you improvise that.

"In the end the blues are not the paper they're written on; it's the horn and the slapped bass, it's the singer and the voice, it's the smoke in the room, it's the people listening, bent forward and eyes closed or shiny, it's the time and place and the ache inside that matches the ache in the words and music. It isn't something to take apart too much—to try and analyze like the amount of butter-fat in milk. It's just:

When I got up this mornin'
Blues walkin' round my bed,
I went to breakfast—
The blues was all in my bread . . ."

Oh, come and buy now
I'm here today
Tomorrow I'll be gone . . .
GRAVEYARD FLOWER SELLER

Black berries
Black a black berries
Pretty black beans
Pretty black beans
O watermelon now
Watermelon now.
NEW ORLEANS STREET CRY

Chapter 6

The Classic Jazz

It took a bit of time to get there, but the classic jazz—as they call it now—came together and jelled and the pure stuff appeared first in New Orleans, and then it spread out like a gambler's card hand. It didn't just happen, and when it was there a lot of people liked it and played it. But that didn't mean it was easy. Most people didn't care for it or want it, and what are called the respectable folk held out against it until the time of bootleggers and the first radios and the flappers and jelly beans of the Jazz Age. But that was much later.

The early times and the hard days and the blue nights of jazz struggling through came earlier. It's hard to get dates and hard to check names, but it's worth it because you can't write a history on only results, you have to find sources. The early writers of jazz—mostly in Europe—confused real jazz with popular ragtime and later Tin Pan Alley jobs, and some wrote learned books on the wrong music.

By 1890 the classic jazz was here, and the New Orleans bands were growing. The small string bands—the combinations of fiddle, guitar, mandolin, string-bass and sometimes piano—were not top dog anymore. They had played popular stuff—waltzes, quadrilles, light classic and when they could handle it, operatic potpourri. It was styled sweet and legitimate and far from the stuff Buddy Bolden and his boys were pouring on at Franklin Street. Of course, the sweet bands did syncopate a bit but it wasn't jazz.

The percussive instruments—the tuba and snare, the bass drums—were the rhythm section when jazz grew up. The clarinet player would ride into a fantastic glissando, going from register to register, and with a little flutter-tonguing that got low-down and dirty. The trombone took the bass and harmony for rhythmic phrases and also the smear of the glissando, almost making a chorus with his private melodies. Often these variations on a basic melody would harmonize in polyphony.

A little changing would turn popular stuff like *Isn't It Hard To Love* into the jazz of *If I Ever Cease To Love*. The trombone had become tail-gate, a fancy sliding parade style, and as "the trombone often sat on the tail-gate of the wagon parading the streets," the style had a name. It was only around 1900 that the piano got into the act with any real results.

So archaic jazz grew up into classic jazz and just where the weld is, it's hard to find. But the change happened. It was almost pure Negro music, with a little white ragtime mixed in, and some Italian opera. New Orleans had grand opera by 1837. You can still catch a ghost of an aria in some of the modern trumpet phrases—say something related to *Rigoletto*.

The Negroes who were playing jazz were close to French and Spanish and Italian cultures. The *tango* and *habanera*—just like the later *samba* and *conga*—drifted out of the Caribbean and into jazz. "Pure" jazz doesn't exist, and it never did. It was all a great melting together of musical cultures performed and improvised by Negroes.

But as any of the followers will tell you, the great band of the period was Buddy Bolden's. He had started as Kid Bolden, and became King Bolden, and just under him was the Excelsior Band, the Indian, Columbus and the Diamond Stone bands. Born just after the Civil War, Bolden dominated them all. "You can only say he was

a freak, a genius, who saw a new way of doing a thing and did it with a remarkable ear and head and lip." He reshaped the prevailing forms of music, took the tendencies and added them up as jazz. You can't explain him or the why and how; you could try but it's better to just admit he existed and did great things because he was a master of the form. He played with a band of five to six pieces—the usual jazz combo. His early group was Buddy at the cornet; Frank Lewis, clarinet; Willy Cornish, trombone; Tom Adams, violin; Tab Cato, bass viol; Brock Humphrey, guitar, and Lou Ray at the traps. They played every place—the Masonic and Globe Halls, at picnics, and downtown at Economy Hall and Hope Hall. And at Come Clean, Provider, Love and Charity and the Big Easy.

"Buddy never rested. He trained his boys, he expanded the styles and the archaic forms. They set the pattern of how to come to jazz and how to play it. Later someone added a piano to jazz, but not much else in the way of using the tools. It was a great time and Buddy Bolden lasted until they locked him up—but as we said, by that time, the music was in and was good. His job was done."

Then there was Bunk Johnson. "This Bunk Johnson, he was a kind of Dan'l Boone of jazz. He was born in New Orleans, around 1879. Nobody was ever sure of the date. At seven he was studying music and soon playing the cornet. At fifteen he was blowing in the band of Adam O'Levy (Oliver). Later, in short pants, he joined the great Bolden band as second cornet. He toured with Holecamp's *Georgia Smart Set,* a minstrel show, and they hit New York City in 1903, Frisco in 1905. He played circus and anything at hand." Fifteen bands used him including The Eagle Band (Bolden's old band under Frankie Dusen). "And that year, the year old Buddy Bolden died, 1931, Bunk had trouble: His trumpet was lost and his teeth fell out and he couldn't lip anything proper any more. He worked in rice and sugar fields in Louisiana, forgotten and lost to music. In 1939, some professors of jazz dug him up, popped a new set of teeth into his mouth, and with a new trumpet he played as well as ever"—a grand old man of jazz. He was always clear and melodic and maybe he showed the dissonant playing of the great classic style, but it was part of the man and his era, and it came from the styles of the marching bands. He is best heard in *Panama* and the *Bogalusa Strut*.

"So the music grew and talent was cheap and sometimes a horn could be bought for a buck in a hock-shop. The honky-tonks and cat-houses were putting in small combos now to please the customers. Boom times in jazz were on . . . and mostly in Storyville, the red-light district.

"If you want it all clean and pure, and not close to vice, you can forget jazz and look for something else. Because in Storyville, classic jazz came of age; had time, money and a place to pour it out, fit it together, and make it good—make it solid. If Jazz is an art form, it happened there. . . ."

end

Keep a'knockin' but you can't come in.
I hear you knockin', but you can't come in.

I got an all-night trick again;
I'm busy grindin' so you can't come in.
If you love me, you'll come back again
Come back tomorrow at haf-past ten . . .

BAWDYHOUSE BLUES

Chapter 7

The Real Storyville

It was maybe the oldest profession and, perhaps, by the end of the nineteenth century, it was being ruined by amateurs, but New Orleans was proud *and* ashamed of its cathouses. It bragged about them, and their girls, and advertised them. And shook heads and counted up the profits at the same time.

"The jazzman could have gotten along without the Madames and their parlours and he didn't have to be part of the sinful livin'. It just happened that way. He had the music and they had the need. He wasn't any more sinful or lustful than anyone else. He maybe just seemed so because he was on the spot. He didn't waste it—but he was there to play the ragtime and the blues and the jazz. That was his job and he did it."

There are the legends that the girls loved him best—"and maybe there were some who doubled in stud. But it was a business in the grind-mills and it took money, and the jazzman wasn't ever too flush." The big money went to the respectable banks and churches who owned the land, and the cribs and the houses with the mirrored rooms and the beds with red plush hangings. The hard work remains today a poor folk's trade and a rich man's pleasure.

"New Orleans liked to think of itself as a city of mighty sinning. It was never ashamed of it, much, but the sin was slopping over by 1897 into the respectable sections of the town. It was time, the best people said, to fence it in and keep it away from the expensive parts of town." In 1897 the blue-noses and the shocked, the church-folk and the remains of the great families started talking it up and the newspapers (whose staffs and editors spent a lot of time in the sporting houses and saloons) couldn't do anything but act shocked and print a lot of mealy-mouthed stuff they didn't believe. Alderman Sidney Story—he seems to have been a respectable man—initiated the ordinance that set up two areas in town where prostitution could be carried on legally. It was prohibited, at least by law, anywhere else.

"One section that was reserved as happy-hunting-grounds for the Madames was uptown, and its boundaries were Perdido and Gravier Streets, and Franklin and Locust. This section never amounted to much. But the downtown section—in the French Quarter—bounded by Customhouse and St. Louis Street and North Basin and Robertson was named, ironically, by the inmates and their sports for the Alderman, and became the famous Storyville. In all it held almost forty lively and jumpy blocks of vice and music, likker and laughter."

For twenty years the tenderloin along famous Basin Street was to mother jazz and make it grow. Storyville became and stayed the biggest tourist and sport-trap in the nation. Tom Anderson became unofficial mayor of Storyville in his City Hall, the Arlington Annex Saloon. He printed and sold *The Blue Book* at a quarter a shot, a full directory and guide of the sporting-houses, listing the names of the working girls and the entertainers to be found in the houses. The Madames took fancy ads in the Blue Book, making remarkable claims for their talented inmates, and picturing the interiors of their extravagantly furnished places. "The big five-dollar house on Basin Street was Josie Arlington's, done in plush and tapestries, leopard-skin rugs and cut crystal chandeliers. Every house had a piano player and often a trio. Singers and dancers spun and made fun and music for the girls and their guests." The first pianist on record hired in Storyville was for Countess Piazza's *maison joie*. His name, he claimed, was John the Baptist. Later Tony Jackson took over the keys on the ivory floor, and his big hit song was *I've Got Elgin Movements In My Hips With Twenty Years' Guarantee.* One of the first blues singers to sing in Storyville was Ann Cook, also featured at the red-lighted number of Countess Willie Piazza.

On Basin Street was the Mahogany Hall, of song and legend, run by Lulu White, called by all the Diamond Queen. "She had 'em every place but in her nose. She also had a mirror-room and the most beautiful octoroons that were known as far west as Frisco. Lulu kept a good piano and for her at various times thumped Al Cahill, Clarence Williams, Richard Jones. Williams did the home-plate an honor by creating *Mahogany Hall Stomp*."

A thirteen-year-old kid came in from Gulfport and went to work for Tom Anderson's Annex where there was usually a good solid trio at work. "He was called 'Jelly Roll Morton' and if he wasn't called Jelly Roll yet, he soon got the name in Storyville. He hit a mean piano and was the maker of the *King Porter Stomp*."

Storyville was a wild place after dark—the big mansions throbbing with subdued music early in the evening before things got hot, the miserable naked girls in the twenty-five and fifty-cent cribs, the lavish brothels looking down at the two- and four-bit trade. And every place the players of jazz perfecting their art. They played in parades and at church burials by day, and in joints in Storyville at night. Cribs, saloons and houses of assignation grew to like the new music as their own, and they liked it because it was honestly sensual, with no shame and furtiveness nor erotic grimace. So it was jazz that gave the rhythm to Storyville and it was Storyville that brought to jazz vice, drink, and later, marijuana. The life was fast, crude and evil, and the jazz and swing-players—from a slice of society already depressed and pushed around—became more maladjusted to normal society. Negro or white, the air that jazz grew up in was tainted and to try and hide this fact as some writers on the subject do is to tell only part of a great story.

"The jazz-player started young. If he had the beat in him, had the flow of the stuff in his blood, he'd joined a kid's spasm band with homemade stuff or toys that you played on sidewalks to sound like the professionals." A lot of good boys were to come out of these sidewalk bands of earnest hungry youngsters trying to collect a few coins from the fumbling drunks, the people hanging around the saloons and honky-tonks.

There was plenty of material to create jazz out of in the two-hundred pleasure joints of Storyville—the cribs, saloons, sinister dancing-schools, the barrel-houses, the creep dives, the honky-tonks and gambling setups. On Franklin Street the big cabarets were led by the *101 Ranch,* at first the hangout of the roustabouts, the pimps and the big gamblers. As it got fancier and the games paid off bigger to the house, a good orchestra and entertainers were brought in. The best of New Orleans showed their talents here. Names only now—Joe Oliver, Baquet, Bechet, Perez, Roy Palmer, Pop Foster, and many others who were to become later part of the New Orleans "Rhythm Kings," "The Halfway House," and "Original Dixieland Jazz Band."

"On Iberville was the *25 Club* where the boys hung out and blew spit from their horns and went on the sauce. You could meet a girl here, a chippie or singer or entertainer in some Storyville dive, the piano usually busy with somebody giving it out for free and a cutting contest would start and some of the boys would jam. It was an exchange for new tunes, old gossip, restful or headachy, the way you wanted it. Pete Lala had a place that used the best boys: Zue Robinson, Joe Oliver, Henry Zino. Kid Ory ran a band there for a spell. So did Oliver, and when Oliver tried on Chicago and there was a spot open for a good horn man, why Louie Armstrong he came in on Oliver's sayso."

The first piano with a band was, most likely, around 1900, under a tent on Iberville Street—Jack White's it was called, a cabaret under canvas. "The piano-player was Black Peter, who couldn't play a tune but chorded along and filled in rhythm. The real gyp joints were the dance schools, the taxi-dance halls and rub joints where the girls danced with whomever stood them a snort. A bottle of beer was a ticket and, brother, were the dances short! There were long time-outs for mauling the girls and buying more drinks. The tonks were pretty blue and raw. A little material that went into jazz came from here. The *28 Club* was a popular river place: pimps and gamblers and tough guys gathered here. You could be taken at faro, three-card monte, and banco. If you wanted exercise, there was crap shooting. It was a blue-playing joint—the blues was the only music for the dives. The words changed a lot but not so often the tune. They had Pig Ankle Night when the host handed out free pig's feet, and Ham Kick Night when a ham was hung high on the ceiling and the gal who could kick highest and show the most leg and thigh got the ham. When a dozen or so gals loaded on likker were kicking at once, a Ham Kick was a wild and dangerous sport."

Bessie Smith, who took part in such contests in her youth, sang a *Pigfoot Blues:*

Check all your razors
An' your guns
We're gonna be wrasslin'
When the wagon comes.

Oh, ain't goin' to do it no more,
Oh, ain't goin' to do it no more.
If I hadn't drunk so much whisky
Wouldn' be layin' here on this hard floor . . .

HARDFLOOR BLUES

Chapter 8

Come Into the Parlor

Americans can never accept vice as part of the human picture. They still listen with their inner ear to the voices of the Puritan past. In protest, to soften their fears, they make of vice a glamour, dress it up fancy and pose it in melodrama and create legends and songs about it. Music in the American scene was more often than not considered a good part of vice. Even the church organ was suspect in many groups. Beyond the voices raised in iron hymns you couldn't see music admitted much as anything but the devil's playmate. The Maypole of New England was burned again and again, and its dancers jailed. The use of music on the frontier and at Hellfire camp-meetings led to many hasty and sudden matings in pine-clearing and wagon-trains. The actress and the singer were considered nothing much more than prostitutes with a sideline. So when Storyville was hustling at its height, "the dirty mean side" took on that legendary lure of sin that is part of the native American dream from New York's Tenderloin district to California's Barbary Coast. And trapped in this native idea of the lure of sin was jazz. Storyville without jazz would have existed, but it wouldn't have sounded the same.

Storyville was jumping those days and when the visitor came out of the Southern Railroad Station on Canal Street, he was looking at Storyville, ready for business, pleasure, vice and jazz. One of the first records in print of a jazz band appeared in an ad for Tom Anderson's Cafe and Annex in *The Blue Book:* "Private dining rooms for the fair sex, all the latest musical selections nightly, rendered by a typical Southern darkie orchestra." Another ad by Countess Willie Piazza brags about her famous Mahogany Hall. "The entire house is steamheated, and is the most handsome house of its kind. It's the only one where you get three shots for your money:

The shot upstairs,
The shot downstairs,
And the shot in the room . . .

If there is anything new in the singing and dancing line that you would like to see while in Storyville, Piazza's is the place to visit. . . ."

Jazz and women were not the only things on tap. A red handbill scattered widely over the town read:

Grand National rat-killing match for $100, to take place at Bill Swan's Saloon, corner Esplanade and Peters Street, third district, Sunday afternoon at four o'clock, precisely . . . a certain New York dog whose fighting weight is twenty-three pounds, to kill twelve full-grown rats per minute for five consecutive minutes.
Admission, 50¢. Reserved seats, $1.

There is no notice as to what music would be furnished at the sporting event.

Many of the ads showed that Storyville had a charm that kept some from bettering themselves musically. Antonia Gonzales advertises how she was kept from fine music.

The above party has always been a headliner among those who keep first-class Octoroons. She also has the distinction of being the only Singer of Opera and Female Cornetist in the Tenderloin. She has had offers after offers to leave her present vocation and take to the stage. . . . Any person out for fun among a lot of pretty Creole damsels, here is the place to have it.

The text does not state if Antonia blew a hot jazz cornet or played old French tunes.

Gimme a pigfoot
An' a bottle of beer.
Send me gate I don't care.
Gimme a reefer
An' a gang of gin
Slay me cause
I'm in my sin.

"It was a hard life knocking out the jazz every night, but the only one you wanted. You started at eight at night and played until the last customer staggered out. You got a buck a night, sometimes two or two-fifty—and a few tips when they let you pass the lid. It was going to last forever, or longer—and the young gals were going to be raised for the trade and there would be chicken and Brunswick stew and corn-pone and pot likker and gumbo for all. And fancy clothes and diamond rings and everything. But one night it was all over. Storyville ended suddenly, like a neck breaking." It was 1917 and America was at war and the moral bluenoses were sniffing around the army camps and keeping our boys pure, so they could make the world safe for democracy. The War Department ordered the full suppression of all "open prostitution." It meant trouble to the Primrose Orchestra, the Magnolia Sweets, Jack Carey's Band and others. The bordello singers didn't believe it. The barrel-house piano kidded the idea. Mayor Behrman of New Orleans went to Washington to protest the closing of Storyville as unsanitary and immoral. But it was no dice; if the city didn't close it, the Army and Navy would.

On October 2, 1917, the Mayor introduced, sadly, an ordinance closing Storyville. It would become law on midnight, November 12. New Orleans would be a clean town from then on. Again sex outside of the home would be done away with for good. A madame, Gertrude Dix, tried for a restraining order, but it didn't work. So the wagons were loaded, the crib girls shouldered their mattresses and walked out of Storyville. The beautiful quadroons wept, and everyone hung one on. "The wet goods flowed. You couldn't move all of it and the jazz boys wrote new blues for the event. The next day all the houses and gals were going full blast in respectable neighborhoods, but music was out for a while."

Countess Willie Piazza was cynical. She said: "The country-club girls are ruining my business!"

"Oh, everybody had them *Basin Street Blues* that last night in Storyville. The brothels sold out or dragged away their beds, padded the mirrors and counted the towels. The Countess sold her big white piano at auction for only a buck-twenty-five. It was a cryin' shame. The place to go was Chicago, a lot said. There was talk of Andrew Volstead and the Prohibition Act, so no more legal boff and soon, no more legal booze. Chicago was close to Canada and maybe it would be the place for the big doings. But everyone was real low. Goodbye, Storyville." Lizzie Green sang its swansong a long time in the *Good Time Flat Blues:*

I can't keep open
I'm gonna close up my shack.
The Chief of Police
Done tore my playhouse down.
No use in grievin',
I'm gonna leave this town.

The legend was to grow bigger than Storyville ever was. "The things they were to tell for years about the place took on a lot that hadn't existed. Jazz itself came of age, and went into Storyville to earn a living, but soon some loose historians were saying jazz had been invented there. They didn't know or didn't care that jazz had come first from the slaves, the marching and burying, the blending of the frontier with African ideas. The other side of the shield is presented by those who just skip Storyville and say it didn't mean much to jazz. You can't have it both ways. The truth is, jazz and vice slept in the same bed for some time. And there was crime, and jazz was part of it."

History (a historian named Gibbon once said) is the recording of the crimes and sins of mankind. "The good and the honest isn't recorded much. So, in jazz, while its records are studded with the crime and vice it has been forced to come to maturity with, there is almost nothing ever said about the pleasant side of it. The people who didn't smoke gage, get razored in barrelhouses and end up being shot in a saloon by a high-yellow girl who said he was her man and he done her wrong."

But a book can't be written about unrecorded histories. Jazz lived in the New Orleans underworld for a long time, and in three special cases it was mixed up with crimes, with matters that brought it to the attention of the nation in a way that made it notorious but helped make the jazz form known.

Basin Street—the original Basin Street—was the red-light street that everyone knew, and the small bands, the piano players, perfected jazz there as much as any place else. "The street got such a bad name that it was broken up later, and the part north of Canal Street was called Crozat and Saratoga Streets, and the part going south to Tulane Avenue was renamed Elk's Place.

For a while there was no Basin Street, but later, some of the downtown part was renamed Basin Street, the City Fathers having felt enough time had passed to make the home of jazz, and jazz itself, something the town could be proud of.

"In the eighties and nineties of the last century the street was wide open. Kate Townsend ran the biggest and highest-priced house at 40 Basin Street. Her ornate parlor served wines, no hard likker, and there was a small jazz-band that played for the lady boarders and their friends. Kate, herself, weighed three-hundred pounds, and she was reported to have the most amazing breasts in town. It was a Frankie and Johnnie setup. She kept a polished Southern gentleman of good family as a lover, had kept Mr. Troisville Sykes (his true name) from work for twenty-five years." Mr. Sykes is described in the newspapers of the time as looking pretty much like Jeff Davis: white linen, small, neat beard, planter's hat, and an ever-smoldering stogie in his face. "Kate felt he had done her wrong one November day and when he came back from drinking bourbon at the corner saloon, she went after him with a bowie knife and a pair of garden-shears. Troisville killed her with her own bowie knife and there was hell to pay along Basin Street. The jazz band didn't play at the house that night and Basin Street hit every front-page in the nation." The press didn't stint in details of life on Basin Street, including its "mad, savage jungle music."

Troisville pleaded self-defense and got off, but the street became known for its bad side from coast to coast. In 1918 after they had closed Storyville and the jazzmen were scattered all over the town and the dance-halls were playing jazz tunes as dance music, a real king-sized crime-wave involved jazz in New Orleans. "You can't find any record of this in any formal history of jazz, but the whole country followed its events with interest, as it was gory, and the first gang killings were not amounting to anything yet." In 1918 a man with an axe appeared one night and chopped in the heads of two people asleep in their beds. He then killed or injured about a half-dozen more people in this manner before a man named Louis Besumer was arrested as "The Axeman." "Because he wasn't married to the Mrs. Besumer who had her head axed in, because he was supposed to be a German spy and because anybody with an accent (he was a Pole and hated Germans) was, as usual, suspected of un-American things, he was jailed. But the murders went on just the same." The jazz boys in the honky-tonks wrote a song about it, *The Mysterious Axeman's Jazz,* or *Don't Scare Me, Papa!* It was a favorite piano piece around town for some time.

In March, the editor of the New Orleans *Times-Picayune* got a letter dated "Hell, March 13, 1919." In part, it read:

Esteemed Mortal,

They have never caught me and they never will. They have never seen me for I am invisible, even as the ether that surrounds your earth. I am not a human being, but a spirit and fell demon from the hottest hell. . . .

There was a lot more of this and why he was killing off people, and a lot about coming from another world. He warned that at 12:15 next Tuesday, he would strike again, *but* that in my infinite mercy I am going to make a proposition to you people.... I am very fond of jazz music and I swear ... that every person shall be spared in whose home a jazz-band is in full swing. If everyone has a jazz band going ... so much the better ... some of those people who do not jazz it on Tuesday will get the axe....

THE AXEMAN

The letter is a historical jazz document for several reasons. It shows that the term "swing" was in use in 1919, well before—as most historians think—the late twenties. It is also one of the rare recordings in writing of early jazz terms—"jazz band in full swing ..." and "a jazz band going" and "people who do not jazz it...." To jazz it is a jazzman's term of the period, not heard much outside of jazz circles. The letter points to the killer having been a jazz player, or hanger-oner.

That Tuesday, *"Don't Scare Me, Papa!* was played on the blue pianos and in the small bands. The whole town played jazz and danced, and waited. The Axeman did not strike that night. Maybe there was enough jazzing in the town to please him. Later a half-dozen more people were killed by the Axeman; even while two men were convicted the axings went on. The convicted men were later freed, the axings still went on and then one day, they stopped. No one was ever axed again in New Orleans—at least, not in the same way." The music of *Don't Scare Me, Papa!* was played for a long time, however. Nobody ever did find out for sure who the Axeman was.

"The average jazzman didn't bother much with crime. He played music and if around him there were blows and bullets, he ducked and sometimes caught one by mistake. Often they took a knife to each other, but the recorded jazz killings don't amount to much....

"Kenneth Neu—a white man—wasn't an important jazzman. He sang in night dives when he could get a job, and he wrote only one bit of music that has come down to us. His main work seemed to be picking up women: he had great charm. And, when out of cash, he committed a few murders."

The cops nabbed him, he wasn't very bright, and he was locked up and convicted, to hang. In the death-house he wrote music dedicated to the hangman: *I'm Fit as a Fiddle and Ready to Hang,* one verse of which reads:

Oh, you nasty man, hanging me
Just cause you can.
But I don't give a good-bye damn,
Oh, you nasty, nasty man.

There exists no record of this music ever having been played. The case made big excitement at the time, not because of the crimes of the singer—they were run of the mill—but because of his handsome face and his real charm. "Women packed the courtroom, and after he was stashed away in the death house, they flooded him with interest. One woman devoted her money and time to seeing him in person and getting him properly set for the next world. He was hanged, and until her death, years later, she placed flowers on his grave on the day he swung off."

If there was one thing jazzmen had, some say, it was charm for the girls. In the dives or in respectable society, the sexual appeal of the jazzman was not just something to hear in song.

"The jazzplayer may have been a good lover, but he certainly was not a true one. In the whole story of jazz the shabbiest side is the romantic one. The jazz boys were poor, usually not too well educated. They had little future and their present was never easy or soft. They took their loving where they found it. When the bands began to carry girl singers, the romances often became famous. Somehow the drummer seemed to be the prime Don Juan of every band. When the combos grew bigger and added a woman piano-player, the tomcatting made history in the form of songs that are still remembered."

One story that's still around is of the jazz band going on a cross-country tour. The leader called up all the men and girl singers and piano players together. "This is a respectable band," he said, scowling. "A real respectable combo, and there ain't goin' to be any immoral horsin' goin' on, you hear me? Whoever you start sleepin' with on this trip, that's how you end the tour! Remember that!"

It is a very human side to the jazz story, showing them as tormented romantics, mixed-up human beings, just as the rest of us are. It's a side of the jazz story most serious historians leave out or gloss over.

But with the closing of Storyville, jazz did come out of the New Orleans underworld, losing almost its best form of earning a living.

It's a long John,
He's a long gone
Like a Turkey through the corn
Through the long corn . . .

LONG JOHN

Chapter 9

They Called It Dixieland

It isn't hard to prove that white men really invented jazz and made it important. It isn't true. But it's easy to prove. A lot of people have been at work saying it. It's the Big Lie of jazz, but a lot of folks who should know better will bet their trumpet on it being so."

There was a white strain of popular music that was close to the roots of jazz. It came from the white poverty, the stark life of the hill-men and the shanty- and shack-boatmen of the bayous and bends. It came from the camp-meetings and the turkey shoots and it was as real and true to the people who made it as the Negro music that was existing at the same time. The two streams weren't pure, weren't kept apart, and each took from the other what he liked, or needed.

"Nobody owned jazz because nobody really wanted it. It was the poor man's tennis and fox-hunt. It didn't take more than a jug, a home-made fiddle, a jews-harp or a wooden sweetpotato. You could cut a flute in no time and the banjo was no problem to transport."

When the white men made music with the Negro stuff, something was bound to happen. For jazz is also the music of white men and the music called Dixieland is the jazz music as the white and black man played it.

"Once, a long time ago, a New Orleans bank put out a ten-dollar bill. On each side was printed the word: DIX. Ten dollars was an impressive sum and you remembered if you got a good ole DIX, a real Southern currency. The word Dixie came from Dix and later Dixie was used in general as meaning the South. But at first Dixie and Dixieland meant *only* New Orleans. So when a white man named Jack Laine began to play jazz, why, they called his music Dixieland."

Jack Laine was born in 1873, and "when he could lift an alto horn off the ground, he began to play it. He also played the drums, but the alto horn was his real love. He played with the rag-time bands, with any white group that worked at the picnics in Algiers across the bend of the Mississippi, at Kramer's Picnic Grounds, at Milneburg on the lake, at the race-track, at fights, and wherever they wanted music. He got connected with the Rappolo family who played a lot of music. Italians and Germans played in the brass bands and at public events . . . and they listened to the Negro bands, but it wasn't until Jack Laine had his Ragtime Band that Dixieland was something new and important." The band had a Rappolo on the clarinet. It also had a cornet, alto horn, drums, and key-trombone. For dancing there was also a guitar, string-bass and violin, but no piano yet.

The band had such men as Achille Baquet, clarinet; Lawrence Vega, cornet; Willy Guitar, string-bass; Dave Perkins, trombone, and Morton Abraham, guitar. "They kicked hell out of *Shadow Rag* and other rags of the period. It was an all-white band to all purposes, even if two light-skinned Negros with blue eyes—Baquet and Perkins—were passing as whites. They all played *Tiger Rag* under a new title, *Praline,* and *Livery Stable Blues* as *Meatball.* They really ragged a tune by their syncopating it. They had neat uniforms and rented themselves out with their outfits for advertising, for things like Ruskin Cigars.

"Dave Perkins passed for years, even if he had once played with Buddy Bolden himself. A white girl fell in love with him. It was a hectic affair. It had to end as there was no solution and, when it did,

Dave went on the booze. He got sick and a colored gal nursed him back to health. Dave married her and that ended his passing. The white music local withdrew his union card."

Laine had a good crying clarinet in Monty Korn, and soon Dixieland music was being played by white bands like Johnny Fischer, Nunez, Massarini and Bill Gallaty. The music was a collective improvisation, with good hard and fast syncopation. Larry Shields was the man who did the best of the new improvisations, very liquid on the clarinet. "He had a sock style making his phrases in bursts with Leon LaRocco's early cornet riding the melody. They had clear vibrant tones when they did *Lazy Daddy* or *High Society*. Today their ragtime may seem too novelty, a little thick with corn, but it was the true beginning of white jazz. J. Russell Robinson, an educated man who could write down music, overlooked his formal background and did *Margie* and *Singing The Blues* for them later." As Nick LaRocca once explained it, "Dixieland was a revolution in 4-4 time."

"Stale Bread Lacoume did a like for jazz, too. He had a kid's spasm band once. Everybody took a fancy name. He played the zither, did Stale Bread Emile August Lacoume, Sr.; Cajun Willie Bussey, harmonica; Whisky Emile Benrod, a half-barrel home-made bass; Warm Gravy Cleve Craven, cheese-box banjo; Slew-Foot Pete Albert Montluzen, soapbox-guitar. They worked like this for Doc Malney's Minstrel Show.

"Stale Bread went blind, but by 1903 he had the band working again with him taking the zither and horn; Dolly Charlie Carey, string-bass; Dude Jimmy Lacoume, banjo; Sweet Potato Harry Carey, tambourine and cornet. They also did riverboats, and worked at Toro's Basin Street. Later, Stale Bread was at Halfway House with Rappolo and Brunies."

The important Rappolo of a large family of jazz players was Leon Joseph Rappolo, born in 1902, at Lutcher, Lousiana. His father played and taught cornet. "Leon took violin lessons from a Negro,

Professor Carrie (not a Harvard professor, but a cathouse piano-player) but he switched to clarinet, stealing his old man's. His father discovered it and sent Leon to a real professor, Santa Guriffe, to learn reading and notes. Ragtime Leon got from Eddie Cherie who was part Negro, passing. At fourteen, Leon ran away to play in a pit-band with Bee Palmer on the Orpheum Circuit.

"At seventeen, Leon was playing with the New Orleans Rhythm Kings, who were about to travel to Chicago to show the nation Dixieland. What a lot of names, and what a lot of replacements. Leon, himself, got into the bright life, went on the smoke, and between the girls and booze and the marijuana, he had a brilliant youth and no future."

It was the story of a lot of jazz pioneers. "It was a tough row, and it got you. The old rale, the sauce, the reefers, or you froze to death in doorways, too stewed to move, or the hacking cough, the shakes; a lot of things happened to the boys. That was Dixieland music; a lot of grief to a lot of men who had a genuine respect for the jazz they took and made their own in their own way. They pushed the beat as all white bands did."

Today they sound fast, jerky, staccato. But they had the real feel, forming syncopation and polyrhythm into repeated one and two measure phrases. The Rhythm Kings relaxed a bit the Original Dixieland style, got it rhythmically closer to Negro beat. You can hear a lot of it in the original *Dixieland Jazz Band* recordings starting in 1917. The Rhythm Kings started recording in 1921. The first big Negro recordings are King Oliver's *Creole Jazz Band* in 1922.

Most of this stuff is acoustically recorded, often by second-rate companies. "They sometimes sold the record as 'Electrically Recorded,' but if you pushed them about that, they admitted they meant the electric-light bulb that lit up the recording chamber." The clarity and balance is often very good. Some of the purists swoon over this as compared to modern recordings made with special seating and extra microphones. They claim modern sides are unnatural and muddy.

But this is usually nonsense, even if there is something to be said for the early unfancy recordings, the theory being that a microphone is an ear and if there are too many ears listening to a playing, it becomes distorted. But, as any engineer can tell you, this doesn't have to be so.

It still sounds very good in the recordings made by *Sam Morgan's Jazz Band* and *Louie Dumaine's Jazzola Eight.* The polyphony is pretty good, well-integrated and only the piano is really hit hard by acoustical recording and lost in the background. Other good recordings are by *Halfway House Orchestra* on Columbia and *Tony Parenti's Famous Melody Boys* on the old Okeh red label. "Dixieland never was a mere hybridization of western music and Negro jazz. All men are brothers, the spirituals sang, all flesh is grass. So what was handy and around makes folk-art, and Dixieland is still alive today. Like everything else, it has its tricky flashy forms and grandstand players. But music isn't as racial as blue eyes and a musty membership in the D.A.R."

It was pretty much set by 1917, pretty much Dixieland by the time the big trek started for Chicago. Soon that was the place to be, "the place where there was money for jazz, night-clubs and torch-singers and roadhouses where later the big bootleggers threw it around, where the torch-singers were to give out with great blues, where a jazzman could live and make his music. And have a session now and then with his friends. It wasn't a healthy city and the booze was bad (Just off the boat, buddy).

"It was a cold dirty town but with a flavor and a juice of its own, and if you froze in doorways, slept in bug-joints, got taken by demanding dames, there was always a way to blow it out of your horn as music.

"And the boys you knew on Basin Street, out at the lake, had horsed with in Storyville, they were around Chicago a lot. The riverboats had brought some a long time ago on excursions, the closing of Storyville had brought others. And last, not least, moola, the money to be had for playing it was up-river along the lake front. As early as 1912 they had drifted in—a cornet in an old sock, a string-bass battered, but game. And by 1917 there were enough of the boys for a club big enough to make a few people understand what you were trying to do with the notes that never got written down."

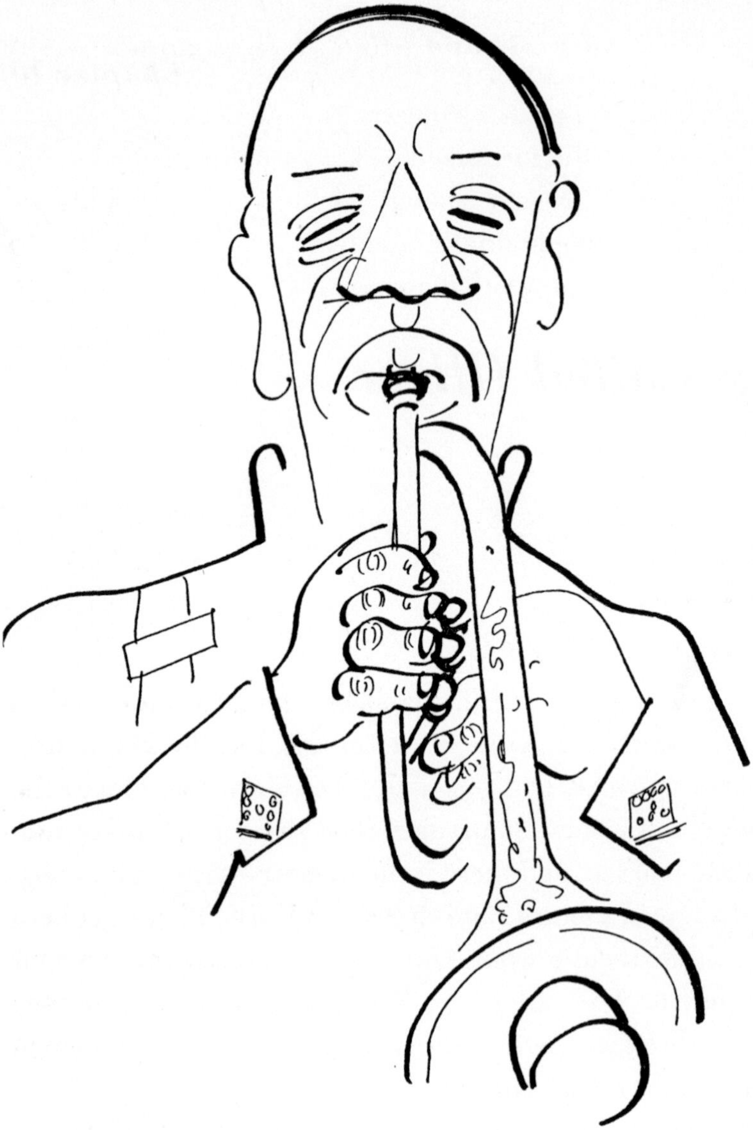

I want to be somebody's baby-doll,
So I kin get my lovin' all the time.
I want to be somebody's baby-doll
To ease my mind.
He kin be ugly, he kin be black,
So long as he kin Eagle Rock
And Ball the Jack . . .

BABY DOLL

Chapter 10

A King Called Oliver

A pioneer is the character who goes ahead on his own, does all the hard work, kills off the Indians, loses his kids in fires and raids, makes the maps, and gets it all taken away from him by the slick Johnny-Come-Latelies. Sometimes they paint a picture of him on a wall no one looks at, and there is the pioneer—drawn all wrong.

"It's the fate of pioneers and they never learn. They can't help it. Something inside them is wound up to go and keep going. To do it the way they feel it. They are better than most people because they see clearer, and they lack, mostly, the ability to live respectable, high off the hog, and make a buck and keep it.

"Joseph Oliver was a great pioneer. The biggest names in jazz today (that doesn't mean the most important) play his stuff without credit, nach, and not one out of ten people who say they like jazz can tell you three facts about him.

"People mourn the passing of the buffalo, and (now that he's pretty much dead) the Indian. They speak of the beautiful wild savannahs and the carrier pigeon, but not of Joe Oliver."

The Garden District is not in the French Quarter of New Orleans. It's in a section of its own and the old eating-place, The Commanders' Palace, is still standing and you can eat the most famous and certainly the best turtle-soup in the world there. "But Joseph Oliver wasn't born that fancy, in 1885. He grew up on Dryades Street, and his family moved around the way colored folk did, hunting a place to get settled in." They did set down at last at Nashville and Coliseum Avenue. "It was a great big time for jazz. Buddy Bolden was high man and Bunk Johnson was setting the cornet style. Joe Oliver, as a kid, played in a child's brass band. He was slow to learn music, which means the written stuff, the old way of putting it down and playing it. When he was about fifteen, the boy's brass band went on tour, going by steamboat to Baton Rouge. It was a tough time for touring Negro bands and there were fights. Joe came home with a knife scar over one eye which he didn't talk about much. He was getting too big for kid bands, and other jobs were hard to get, so he became a butler for white folk.

"But the music still burned in his mind and Joe played around with his horn in the servants' rooms, very mute, and not letting out. He played around in bands, and the white folk didn't mind and let him train a boy to take his place when he had to play. He tried out with the Eagle Band but they said he was loud and bad. The Eagles didn't worry over written-down music, and Joe Oliver had been impressed by the written-down so he couldn't fly high with them. But then he got the whack of it, he liked it fine, it was his kind of thing. So he buttled and played at Negro funerals and he worked out a variation on the old hymn *Sing On* that nobody wanted to miss when they got buried. Joe worked hard and listened to Bunk Johnson play and he worked out a stomp of his own, *Dippermouth,* and that was his trade-mark for a while. Everybody used to shout out for Joe to give them *Dippermouth.*"

Joe crossed Canal Street, getting out of the butler belt, and joined Manuel Perez' *Onward Brass Band.* "Joe really could blow it and in no time at all he was playing in Storyville, his horn wide open and roaring, just like the place. He played with the Aberdeen Brothers, in a joint corner of Bienville and Marais, with Big Eye Louie,

Deedee Chandler, Dick Jones. Joe began to blow it big in B-flat and one night he just walked out of the dive and right into the street blowing that horn better than ever, and the whole street stopped to listen and no one had ever done it like that before, they all said."

He was King Oliver from then on, and led his own band at Lala's Cafe. It was some band, with Lorenzo Tio, Zue Robinson, Buddy Christian and Zino. Lala's became the place to hear some of the best of the stuff. "Jazz lovers, tourists, the sporting-men, all came to Lala's to hear King Oliver blow his horn in gully-low stomps and the real blues. Later, when the night was over for the customers, the Storyville players would drift over to Lala's and put on a session of their own, Joe blowing with them, the music getting newer and more different, everyone taking turns in trying out his ideas. And that's how jazz grew a little more in the dirty streets, with the river smells and the marsh stinks; and the chalky mist from the river at morning finding a lot of tired jazzmen going home to get some shuteye."

When they closed Storyville in 1917 there were a lot of old New Orleans men who couldn't get work and among them was King Oliver. So he went north and among the first public playing he did in Chicago was under the El trains in the Loop playing tail-gate trombone from a wagon to get people to buy Liberty Bonds. They put on their New Orleans jass (not jazz) on Wabash Street. He was also indoors playing at two South Side joints. His *Creole Jass Band* playing the *Royal Garden Blues* set his style, and he was one of the sights of Chicago just like Al Capone, the corner where the daily gangster was put on the spot, and the Charleston contests.

King Oliver liked Chicago, but he didn't change much. "He remained a horn player from the south, eating his big plate of hominy, and now that he could afford it a half-dozen hamburgers and a quart of milk as his idea of lunch. And if any man wanted a pie-eating contest, he was ready." There is a legend he once ate twelve pies at a sitting. Besides food, King liked pool and baseball and kids.

When Joe went to Dreamland, he organized a new band and did something daring—he got a woman, Lil Hardin, to play the piano and she wasn't from New Orleans. Lil Hardin needs a little telling herself. She got to Chicago from Memphis around 1917, to go on studying music in the Fiske University style. But somehow she got crossed up with jazz, and she stayed and liked it. Oliver also hired Honore Dutrey, Minor Hall, Ed Garland and Johnny Dodds.

"They played every night, 9:00 to 1:00, and then packed up the stuff and moved seven blocks down to the Pekin Cafe, to go on from there. The Pekin was always exciting, full of spenders, bootleggers, killers and thrown bottles. The reek of bathtub booze kind of gave it a flavor. The golden years were whizzing by for King Oliver, just like the corny song-titles said. The band went on tour, and came back and King had Louie Armstrong come up from New Orleans to play with him.

"They played at the new done-over Gardens; that tall, thin building with scrolls of stone cut into it, with its facade, and the balconies looking down on Thirty-first Street. A real eyesore, with its arches and full of all the fancy mugs and the low sports and the best people all coming to hear King Oliver and Louie play their horns.

"It was no joint for respectable fox-trotting or waltzing. If you danced, you tried on the Bunny Hug, the Black Bottom and the Charleston. The stompings were regular and popular, King Oliver tooted his horn, the beat got started, Lil hit the keys, the drums and the rest moved up and when Joe and Louie stepped forward to blow their breaks, the place was jumping.

"Nobody used much written-down music, just a few marked-up sheets with the titles torn off (so no one could swipe the stuff too easy). It was a hard time to keep your stuff your own. Everybody was coming in and borrowing from King Oliver. The Dixieland boys at Friar's Inn had helped themselves to *Jazzin' Baby Blues,* playing it under a new handle as *Tin Roof Blues.* Joe and Louie went on with their duets, and everybody got involved in improvisations. Dutrey's trombone style was right up there with the leaders. He changed the trombone's job and used it to back up the rhythm action."

They were beginning to make records now for Gennett, in a little studio that wasn't all it should be, but was good enough to make some fine sides when they moved Joe and Louie twenty feet back from the recording horn to keep from wrecking the joint. Louie did his first record solo, *Chimes Blues.*

They made some records later for Columbia and after that the band kind of broke up. Louie was getting too strong, they said, for King Oliver to have around. The King was recording with other players and still calling it the *Creole Jazz Band.* So after a tour through the Middle West, Louie left King Oliver. "Joe Oliver was slipping. He was running into some hard luck, but he took it in his stride. He never changed much, even when the going got real hard. He played as well as ever, and ate as big as ever, when he could afford it. His heart was his horn and his music. Give him a chance with both, he could be happy."

The Defender carried an ad in September, 1924:

AT LIBERTY: The celebrated KING OLIVER'S JAZZ BAND—8 men playing 15 instruments. Open for engagements in or out of Chicago. Joseph Oliver, 3033 South State Street, Chicago.

"Things were going bad. The Gardens burned down on Christmas Eve, just when Joe was getting together a new band to open there. He was still billed as 'the world's greatest jazz cornetist' when he went to play at the Plantation Cafe with *Peyton's Symphonic Syncopators.* But it wasn't the same. Peyton kind of rubbed it in when Joe lit a cigarette between numbers. 'You can't smoke here in my band. You smoke outside when you're working for me.' This was a new way to talk to King Oliver. But he didn't protest; he knew times weren't so good for him.

"Things picked up a bit later. He got together a band and they played at Crane College, and they made some records as the

Dixie Syncopators. They were good; the *Sugarfoot Stomp,* the best. But they weren't just like the hot jazz King Oliver had done in the old days. Times were getting tough for jazz players, by 1927. The real depression wasn't to hit the country until 1929 with the Republicans' nice fat words for keeping calm. But jazz felt it long before the rest of the country. Joe got into the music publishing field, 'office hours, two to four every afternoon.' Joe was writing down all the things in his head, putting down what he remembered, things of his own when jazz grew up. He and Lil Hardin arranged them and got a copyright and published some of it. They did a fine job and saved a lot of what was best in King Oliver's music, what made it so original and important.

"But Joe couldn't keep out the borrowers who never gave him credit for his music when they stole it. He owned *Camp Meeting Blues,* which didn't stop Duke Ellington from recording the theme as *Creole Love Call,* with no credit to Joe, of course. Ellington and Miley and Rudy Jackson were listed as its 'composers.' A man named Mezzrow, a Jew passing as Negro, took the theme of Joe's *Dippermouth* and copyrighted it under his own name as 'composer-arranger,' titled *Apologies.* Bob Crosby's band made a side called *Dixieland Shuffle,* which isn't much different than Joe's *Riverside Blues.* King Oliver's name isn't on any of these things, yet they are his. So that's how some of the early jazz history got fouled."

The Plantation closed in 1927 and Joe sent out letters:

> I am at leisure should you . . . have anything to offer I would highly appreciate any favor you render. Respectfully yours, Joseph Oliver.

Joe went East to play two weeks at the Savoy Ballroom in Harlem. "After that he played around, turned down the Cotton Club, found out a lot of music was being played below scale in New York and Joe didn't play that way. Things got worse and he was down to one-night stands in Brooklyn, Newark, Asbury Park. Joe was as good as ever. He and the boys did some recordings for Brunswick, but a cold wind was abroad in the world. Times were not getting better."

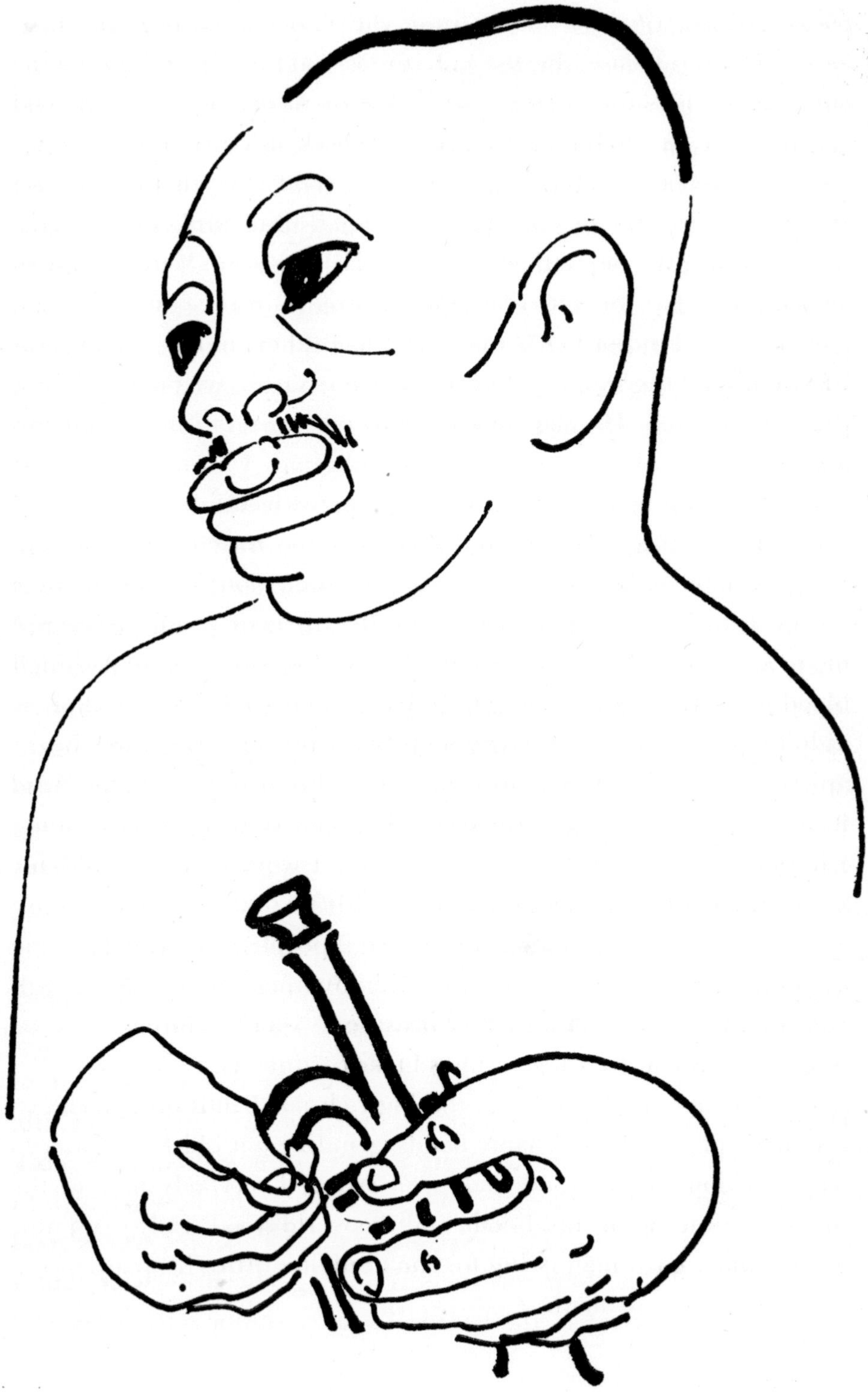

All this time, he was helping with money, publishing music, aiding Harlem talent, always ready to see good music and good men encouraged. But after making some Victor recordings, "he got paid off on a tour for the boys with a rubber check and dirty unfair agents took big cuts out of him. 1931 was not a good year for the country. Joe tried tours and the band got stranded, dead broke, in whistle-stops. After that he settled down in Huntington, West Virginia, owned a bus and for four years played around in the country. Then a frost split the motor block and after Joe fixed the motor, the bus was wrecked. Lawyers hounded him for a year over the accident and then the big blow fell. He had no money to take care of himself and his teeth went into pyorrhea, and out they all came. A horn man without teeth is no horn man at all. And good store teeth cost money."

It was tough going from then on—the rotten little tours in 1937, no money, landlords screaming for their dough, broken-down busses, penny-pinching, and worst of all, an agent trying to sell the name *King Oliver's Band* to someone else. Joe was sick. He had high blood-pressure now, real high, and treatments cost money and he didn't have any cash. The treatments, he wrote, only cost three bucks apiece, "but where was it to come from? From the big name band leaders who were piling in the jack using some of King Oliver's music without his name on it? The world doesn't work that way, and Joe knew it. He was down and only needed a little scratch for treatments.

"His last letters break your heart, if people still mean anything to you. To a sister, he writes: 'Should anything happen to me, will you want my body? Let me know because I won't last forever and the longer I go, the worse I'll get unless I take treatments.'

"That's the way it was, the big rich jazz-bands of America in the smart places, the big name bands, grinding out old King Oliver's stuff, making it sweet and making it swing. Everybody now in the money as times went into boom, and the world stood ready to go nuts again. And a good man dying for the need of a little cheap attention, three dollars a treatment."

This man—Joe Oliver—was a true artist, a pioneer in a fine art form, a man—the first—who really worked in moving it out of New Orleans and taking it north and spreading it around. But there was nobody to save Joe Oliver, even if they were replaying his music every time you turned on the radio. He wrote: "Don't think I'm afraid because I wrote what I did. I am trying to live nearer to the Lord than ever before. . . . Good night, dear."

Two months later—April 10th, 1938—he was dead. "His sister spent her rent-money to bring the body to Woodlawn. But there was no money left over to buy a gravestone. There still isn't any money to buy that gravestone for the unmarked grave."

Chicago, Chicago,
That toddlin' toddlin' town.
Chicago, Chicago
I'll show you around . . .

CHICAGO

Chapter 11

That Wide Open Town

Jazz wasn't always lucky in the places it had to settle in and grow, but in New Orleans and Chicago it got a lot of action for its money. They were both—and still are in many ways—frontier towns. They go armed and they pull the gun and they kill a lot of each other. They live proud of their dirt and their gangs, proud of their city, and even, every so often, their crooks in office. They like the idea of stealing and making your pile and growing bigger and having a tough past. Just as the shame of the cities never fazed New Orleans, Chicago developed a proud shrug that seemed to say: What the hell, kid. Live and let live. Let's make a buck and have some fun.

"You can't imagine jazz getting any place in Richmond or Seattle. It had to be a town where the dyin' was easy, the money come by without hard work, and the citizens not too much in love with easy odds. Bring in some music, a new kind of music, played by characters you wouldn't care to bring home to mother, let it have a beat and zing that put life into a lot of what you feel, and some of what you think, and it's bound to catch on sooner or later.

"So Chicago was a good place, and a bad place, too. And, like a germ-culture, at least you could live off it for a while if you stayed out of the way of the big killers. But it wasn't the place for jazz folk to raise up a family, be respectful to women or keep a bank account."

Chicago is proud and dirty, fast, and with a roar all its own. From rotting Dearborn Station with loud-speakers pouring schmaltzy music over the sooty heads of the waiting-room mob, to the Lake Front, all glass and copies of copies of Paris styles, it has a flavor of its own. The jazz world was also a special part of the town and no matter how much of it leaked out as it spread its music among the natives, much of the jazz in Chicago is connected with a few places and names.

"The town is big, wide in the rump along Lake Michigan with a sewer called the Chicago River marching right through the town, bending enough to make the district called the Loop full of El trains, strip tease, burlesque dives full of bump-and-grind types. And very fashionable shops. M. Fields and all the rest."

The Negro part of town is south of the Loop between the lake and stockyards. It wasn't as comfortable or fancy as living on Lake Shore Drive or Detroit's Grosse Point. "Moving down State Street from the Loop you came to the sporting section, the cathouses around 22nd Street, and the little dives where they early began to play jazz. The players all shaking from the cold lake breeze blowing through their torn shoes and patched pants. There were fancy places, too, at night, anyway: Pony Moore's and the Everleigh Club. They had piano-players, small ragtime outfits. The boys came and went.

"From 1910 on you could hear Bennie Harney, Tony Jackson, Jelly Roll Morton, playing in the houses and sometimes at places like the Elite, or Dago and Russell's.

"It was a tough town to play in but it had a flavor. There were tinny upright pianos with a kitty to feed the music-maker, and some of the good boys came up later with names like Joe Oliver, Fred Keppard, but it was mostly just 'nigger music' and 'whorehouse music' to the smart advanced people who move in on everything new in the arts, when all the suffering and hunger is over and the thing is about ready to bust wide open, anyway.

"You could jazz it at the Grand Theater, Thirty-first and State. It was all over—good and hot and solid, but tucked away and forgotten. They called it 'creole music' at first, all Negro music in Chicago was called that for some time.

"You played it in cold-water flats, at Kelley's Stable across the sewer from the Loop, in the street-corner speaks, in the red plush parlors of madames, at the Entertainers' Cabaret where a Singer Midget piano was on wheels and a guy named Earl Hines played it and pushed it around.

"Nobody liked to sleep much so you sat around and jammed or went to the buffet flats in the old Ellis Building and talked and drank and played the old-style orthophonic Victrolas, those arm-cranking things like the Model-T Fords.

"It was a small tight and smoky world at Calumet and Thirty-fifth Streets, where you talked with a fag hanging from your tired lip, the horn wrapped in newspapers under your arm, while the yellow girls stood around giggling and the sellers sold unlabelled gin.

"Everything was jazz. The Sunset and the Plantation were big names (not yet so big) and played it very good. Yes, it came early to Chicago, but it had to wait a while, wait a bit before the big numbers in jazz came along and blew it so loud they blew it right out of Calumet and Thirty-fifth, right all over the whole city. . . ."

By 1900, to go back a bit, the jazzmen were already moving north and east and west—not in great numbers, not an organized invasion, just driftin', just followin' the river and roads "looking for a dollar, a place to play some music." The riverboat that had seen Mark Twain, and the good living and the fancy dress and the packets with "niggers to burn and blow up" (when the safety valve was held down in the golden days of river steaming), were turning into cheap excursion steamers and show-boats. *The Capitol, The St. Paul, The Sidney* and what remained of the big river fleets carried passengers and jazzmen to St. Louie, Memphis, Cairo and Davenport. The suck of the major tributaries swirled muddy against their bows and thrashing paddle-wheels breasted the Ohio as far as Pittsburgh, the Missouri up to Kansas City and Omaha. They went tooting into the Red River and the St. Joe, and down the delta, past Algiers Point, and into the Gulf and along the bayous choked with river flowers and 'gator snouts.

"It was dancing, singing, eating and loving, riding on the rivers with orchestras, steam calliopes, and Negro bands. Louie Armstrong played in the river bands, and Fate Marable organized them out of St. Louie. Good men and great like Pop Foster, Baby Dodds, Johnny St. Cyr, played on muddy waters; sometimes sweet, but, as often as they could, jazz. You carried a hot trumpet and a sweet trumpet, and you played twelve numbers every three hours; two of these numbers were usually the freest, hottest jazz there was."

And so on the boats the jazzmen drifted into Chicago. By 1915 Sugar Johnnie and Roy Palmer and Larry Duke were doing vaudeville in Chicago. A year or so later they were playing the DeLuxe Cafe on the South Side with such people as Lillian Hardin, the non-New Orleans jazz pianist, Wellman Breaux Braud, bass, and Ram Hall, drums. From 1912 to 1917, the *Original Creole Band* was playing cross-country. A lot of little bands were playing in the Negro section. In June, 1915, the first important white jazz band came: the *Tom Brown Band* from New Orleans opened at the Lamb Cafe. Ray Lopez, Gus Mueller, Arnold Loyacano, Will Lambert made up the band, with Brown, himself, at the trombone.

It was a big hit and people began to talk of "jass" and "whorehouse music," as it was called. BROWN'S DIXIELAND JASS BAND, DIRECT FROM NEW ORLEANS went up on the roof.

Back in New Orleans at the 102 Ranch (formerly the 101 Ranch) there was in 1916 a Dixieland trio—Yellow Nunez, clarinet, Henry Ragas, piano, and Johnny Stein, drums. It came north to Chi with a few men added: Eddie Edwards, Nick LaRocca and Tony Sbarbaro. They appeared at Schiller's Cafe and called themselves *The*

Dixieland Jass Band. The local Dixieland bands merged and mixed and came out as *The Louisiana Five* and *The Original Dixieland Jass Band.* They played at the DeLabbe Cafe and the Duquesne Gardens and every place they made jass popular and notorious.

The white men were first to become popular in Chicago; the black men who had invented it came later. This confused lots of people who accepted and tried to name Dixieland as an original white jazz form not connected with Negro music. The Dixielanders themselves never claimed anything that silly. Negro jazz hit Chicago first in a big way when King Oliver came to Chicago around 1917. And he was Negro music, as far as Chicago read it, until 1924. He brought along his music, things like *Canal Street Blues, Dippermouth* and *High Society.* He held two jobs at once for a while, playing cornet at The Royal Gardens and at Dreamland playing under Duhe in the *Original Creole Band.*

By 1920 he had organized his *King Oliver's Creole Jass Band* (it appears to have gone from jass to jazz around this time). That was also the year the *New Orleans Rhythm Kings* came to Chicago. Oliver had a fine group—Lil Hardin, piano; Ram Horn, drums; Jimmy Noone, clarinet, replaced soon by Johnny Dodds.

"The town was jumping, bootleggers were appearing and growing fat and sassy, the first hood had been taken for a ride, alki cutting was a trade, and there was lots of tainted money to spend. The Oliver band played at Dreamland until one in the morning, bundled up and stumbled over to the nearby Pekin Cafe, where the new bigshots, the early mobsters, and the hophead gunmen were showing up, loaded with dough."

King Oliver toured California after that, jitney dances at the Pergola Pavilion in Frisco's Market Street, and at Purcell's Barbary Coast dive. They played in Los Angeles at Leeks' Lake Resort, then gigged around until they got back to Chicago at a done-over Royal Gardens, now renamed Lincoln Gardens Cafe.

"Oliver had left Louie Armstrong behind him in New Orleans, at Lala's, and now he sent for Louie to take second cornet. Louie was twenty-two, strong and eager, kind of a hick. They say he came up from the railroad station, put down his straw suitcase, took out his horn and fell right in with the band, following the King's lead in the second cornet part. Louie was a hit and he and the King knocked out their duets side-by-side, good hot licks and making it solid, and everybody said the King had made a mistake bringing somebody that good north to play with him."

The band recorded with four companies—Gennett, Paramount, Okeh and Columbia. Around thirty-seven sides, acoustic of course, these were the first of great Negro jazz classics cut in wax. They did *Mabel's Dream, Canal Street Blues, Mandy Lee Blues,* and all their favorite numbers. Some experts have played these on a turntable revolving at 33-1/3 r.p.m. to catch hidden details, but this is nonsense; it's to be heard as played at the standard 78 r.p.m.

With *The Rhythm Kings* in town at the Cascades Ballroom, and later at Friar Inn, black-and-white jazz had taken over Chicago. They all stayed up and studied the King and his band; they played Dixieland their own way, and they set up a lot of stuff that was going to influence the budding so-called "Chicago style." Among other converts were such white sweet bandmen as Paul Whiteman who just called himself "The King of Jazz," without bothering to play it, and also Guy Lombardo, another sugar-cornball.

The real Chicago School was started around 1923 and called itself the *Wolverines.* Around 1923 the group made their first recordings with Bix, cornet; Al Gande, trombone; George Johnson, tenor-sax; Jimmy Hartwell, clarinet; Dick Voynow, piano; Bob Gillette, banjo; Min Leibrook, bass; and Vic Moore, drums. "The boys were good, but fuzzy, with no basic beat, only a fast tempo. They were at times a little too highly-arranged, and yet often faked their group improvisation. Bix had a beautiful tone, clear, romantic and plaintive." The purists have never liked the *Wolverines,* saying they were not hot but sweet, sentimental; and some disliked their invention of that jumpy rhythm labelled *vo-de-o-do*. The *Wolverines* certainly couldn't play like Basin Street Negroes, and hadn't the same tempo and outlook as Dixieland players, but to condemn them for trying and doing something well is the kind of thing that has broken jazz up into little private cults.

Everybody doin' fine,
All you folks that ain't in line
Come on out and rise and shine,
Big Apple! Have a bite . . .

BIG APPLE

Chapter 12

"The Jazz Age"

A thing or a group gets a label stuck on it and you can't pull it off. Someone once called something the Holy Roman Empire, and historians prove it wasn't Roman, or holy, or an empire any longer. But that didn't matter, the name stuck. Just so, "The Jazz Age" which ran from right after 1918 to around the middle of the thirties wasn't a pure jazz age, and most of the jazz of the period wasn't good. "The Jazz Age" was wildest from about 1922 until Wall Street laid that egg in 1929.

"By that time, jazz was everyplace and blamed for everything, and the wail of a saxophone (never a really good jazz horn) was the sound of doom to a lot of people. A man named John Held Jr. drew the jazz-flapper and her sheik best, the girl with long, long legs, cropped shingled hair, a cigarette and likker flask in her hand. The lad was apple-headed, his hair buttered tight down. He wore bell-bottomed trousers, a racoon coat, drove a Stutz Bearcat and played or danced to jazz a lot. F. Scott Fitzgerald was the high priest of the literary salons where all the young men drank it away and jazzed it away, and died young and left a beautiful body. He was the writer who recorded the events of the Jazz Age. . . . But he, himself, knew nothing of the real jazz. He stuck to the Ritz."

Jazz didn't change our morals in the late twenties and early thirties. But it furnished the music to a change in manners and sexual ideas. Women wore less, and wore it in a slipping, careless way, on the dance-floors. Legs seen to mid-thighs were no thrill any more. Everyone wore silk-stockings—and many rolled them beneath the knees so that every sitting-down showed the American thigh, nude and lush, anywhere from kneecap to buttocks.

There was more lipstick, and one wondered at its color. Hair was cut short, hung close to the skull; perfume was poured on—and not only among the factory girls and the salesgirls—but on the housewives, the Main Streeters, the rustic society queens, the jazz-bands' blues singers, the diplomats' wives, the lady artists, and the wives of corn-fed congressmen. Jazz seemed the answer to the pulse-beat, the rising sense of revolt.

"Aging wolves acted parts in roadhouse vices, crossroad flappers became chain-smokers. Cigarettes were for ladies now (even the jazzman's reefers) but, of course, not as much in public as in private and at parties. The blue-noses still sniffed at the coffin-nails and the Negro jazz-band, but allowed the cocktail. The ulcerated stomach showed you got enough to drink, tired feet that you could do the jazz-inspired dance-steps. Mixed drinking was the thing. Drinking, not of dinner-cocktails, wines and sweet-scented stuff after coffee, but the flask and jazz-dancehall cloakroom drinking by young girls in their teens. Every dance left at least a half-dozen of the chits—high school girls, debutantes and convent-bred misses—dead drunk in the corners, among the sports, the drifting society tramps, the jazz drummers and horn-players."

High-class parties were no worse than any others. At the cocktail hour the same thing went on in studios full of batik or modern pale versions of Matisse, and a jazzman at the Steinway. It was a time of Freud; but Marx was pushing him hard. And every place one went the rattle of the cocktail shaker was heard, and the *Basin Street Blues*. In hotel bedrooms, girls and men and women and boys lay around on beds and drank themselves cockeyed as those records ground out *Frankie and Johnny.* Country-clubs, summer resorts, were no better. Saturday night left its hangovers across the land. Hips were flask-protected, and everyone matched his partner drink for drink. *"Sugar, you're a sport; let's cut a rug."*

The talk didn't shock any more. Nothing verbal did but one was surprised how far one had come from gutter-dirt, backfence words. Bessie Smith's records, the low-down ones, were collectors' items.

"Sex was the best and most popular subject and it took a terrible beating in real life and in jazz titles. The little girls, looking so sweet and demure, knew all the words from canhouses and *The Meat-Grinder Blues,* and seemed ready to illustrate them with anyone, haunches shaking. *Damn* and *Hell* and *Lousy* and *sonofabitch* were not male words any more. Anyone could use them anywhere. Plays, records, books, helped.

"One ran into the petting parties. One was always stumbling over couples drinking, necking, limbs locked, in an emotion only half understood, but somehow connected with jazz. One knocked on a door before entering a room; one inspected the back of the car for company sitting in the dark; one searched the cloakrooms, closets and spare bedrooms before locking up for the night after a gathering—and one didn't open a lady's handbag unless by mistake. There was a new wisdom abroad. As the whole nation was seized by this drinking, dancing jazz frenzy, the intellectuals either joined in or retreated across the sea to Paris 'where they do this sort of thing with more taste.... Now you take Josephine Baker...'."

So, curved in tight silk, the girls were squeezed everywhere to trumpet-chords. Middle-class morality was dancing to jazz.

Jazz lived in the social whirl, this whole mess of smart people, coming people, rich people, people with something to sell—something to give—something to smear their neighbors with. This world and the underworld kept jazz alive. But the real jazz players knew it wasn't the pure music any more.

Now, hobo, oh, hobo, hobo, you can't ride this train.
Now, boy, I'm a brakeman, and I'm a tough man.
I ain't jokin', you can't ride this train . . .

HOBO YOU CAN'T RIDE THIS TRAIN

Chapter 13

A Folk Hero

Nobody knows how folk heros grow. How we came to accept Dan'l Boone as the symbol of the pioneer. Or how Buffalo Bill came out of the dime-novels and turned out to be only a drunken old man who could stay on a white horse. Sometimes, like Mike Fink and Paul Bunyan, it's just folk talk that gets solid and somebody puts it in a book and claims credit; sometimes it's a lie, like George Washington and the cherry tree, and John Smith being saved by an Indian princess, that sounds so good we can't throw it away. "The folk hero can be anybody—a baseball player, a cowboy actor who chews gum and cracks wise, or a lady like Lizzie Borden who did a murder or two in an interesting way."

Bix Beiderbecke became a folk hero early and he's remained the symbol of the jazz player who wanted something better and died trying to get it. "He's the man Maurice Ravel, the great modern composer, came to New York to see and he and Bix sat around and talked modern music. Once when the society people were giving a big party for Ravel they looked for him and found him hidden in a bathroom rewriting Bix's *In A Mist* so he could catch the ideas behind it." Certainly Ravel was in New York when Bix was, and they may have met and Ravel did say he was impressed by the music. But did he come just to see Bix or rewrite *In A Mist?* You can't prove it, either way.

"But they don't build legends around nothing. They know these legends from the home of the gully-low music to the dives where there is always someone having a ball and borrowing a blip, where the clinkers creep into the mist just before dawn. In Harlem and the Chicago South Side and the Le Jazz Hot joints in Paris where the dicty folk come to hear the bellychords they talk of Bix Beiderbecke. There have been a couple of just-fair novels about him, and once a very lousy movie, not much above simple razzmatazz and the Hollywood idea of jazz.

"The legends aren't very true but they have been growing and there isn't much you can do about it because the guy was good and even those who used to stand around under the bandstand and shout *We want Bix!* are telling myths about him.

"They didn't have to; the facts are plenty and sad and you don't fracture yourself laughing when you hear them."

Leon Bismark Beiderbecke—not the legend—was born; that's a fact. The date was March 10, 1903, the place, Davenport, Iowa, and the riverboats used to go that far with their bands. "His older brother was called Bix, and Leon inherited it from him. No one seemed to mind. His folks had made their pile in lumber and they had culture besides money, and were all a little daffy about music. His sister knocked off a good piano; his mother had studied both piano and pipe-organ and when only ten, had won a medal at it. His grandfather led German-American music in Davenport and his grandmother's father played an organ—Bach and stuff—in Europe.

"Bix never amounted to much of a sight-reader, but he wasn't ignorant, as the legend said. He took some lessons on the piano from a Professor Grade, who seems to have been the real thing. When only three, Bix could play the melody of the *Second Hungarian Rhapsody.* But on the cornet that made him famous, he never took a lesson in his life. He never played it right, just good. He was surprised once to find he was not playing it in the same key as the piano. He couldn't read cornet-parts very well and bumbled along with violin-parts which he found easier reading. He loved the third value on the horn—everybody else used the first two keys most. Not Bix. It was all wrong according to the teachers, but he got a good flow into his horn chords in his own way. He liked the cornet, its full mellow charm, maybe because it was close to the human voice. It had just the sting he wanted and he stayed with it. It tongued easy and one simple mute was enough. Bix didn't put much mute in his legato styling and his round tones were all right without mutes.

"Where did he get his style? From someone else. Every writer or painter starts by copying what he likes best and so did Bix. Don't copy and you're doing the dooley-squat—nothing. Bix did plenty of woodshedding, playing alone, to some recording on the family Victrola, and any white man who didn't in those days is a liar. King Oliver, Louie Armstrong, Bix he knew their recordings as a kid. And LaRocca, too, and maybe Emmett Hardy. Also Paul Mares, Fate Marable and Johnny Dunn."

Bix was close to his mother, maybe too close, only the silver cord never pulled him back from his horn. She remembers him in his teens playing his cornet to LaRocca's recording of *Tiger Rag.* From Oliver and Louie came the off-scale tonality. The riverboats all carried music. There was Hardy, a white horn-man, and the Strekfus line-boat; the *Capitol* had bands with Oliver and Louie in them.

"Bix liked jim-jam singing and moaning low and the real old blues. Bessie Smith and Ethel Waters he remembers, and their phrasing. He was a kid with a horn; a million kids must be like him every place, thinking of what they want to say and copying from hot-stuff and other ways of saying it. Listening to the press-roll on snarls, the newer jumps of the short riffs, and even the rinky-dink bands that played jitney stops around the town. Bix played it all boogity-boogity and learned a lot, and then they sent him away to school.

"Bix did two years in the Davenport High School, then in 1921 was put into Lake Forest Academy on the North Shore of Chicago. New Orleans and Dixieland music was just hitting Chicago and Bix played in the school band, first on the piano and then as a star on the cornet. He didn't get good marks, he hated to study and he was already as a kid (like General Grant as a boy) on the sauce in a charming school-boy way. Everybody loved him and he drank gin and played music and was amiable, but didn't crack a book. They kicked him out and instead of going home, he hung around Chicago, did a few nights gigging and just waited for the *Wolverines* to start in business. He kind of knew his destiny and he never did much to change it. Something would happen and it did.

"The *Wolverines*—bright-eyed and bushy-tailed—opened at the Stockton Club, a dive near Hamilton, Ohio, late in 1923. They were popular and people liked them—which only means that people who liked good jazz heard them. And there weren't a hell of a lot of them. But they knew what they liked, and it was the group around Bix, and Bix himself and his horn. It was a scuffle and had its salty moments and you buried your blues in King Kong, the cheapest whisky there was.

"So there they were—the best white jazz-band in the country next to the *Original Dixieland Jazz Band* and the *New Orleans Rhythm Kings*. Their playing was going to lead to Chicago style and they *vo-do-de-o-doed* maybe a bit too much, but in 1924 it was all right to the early cats.

"There was a guy named Hoagy Carmichael, who was later going to get rich and write popular stuff for the squares and live in Hollywood on a hilltop like a millionaire movie-actor, but in those days he was a big gun on the campus of Indiana University. He got the *Wolverines* hired for a frat-dance without hearing them. Hoagy had a band of sorts of his own on the campus and talk of Bix's boys excited him.

"The music they played that night was enough to bring them

back to the campus for ten weekend dances. After that they played Casino Gardens in Indianapolis, and a summer-theater tour. Bix was really on the booze now, but the idea the legends plant that he could play drunk or sober isn't so. Real drunk, he could only fall on his face and snore. Mildly plastered, he could reach a piano and play, but when he got the bang-up choruses out of the brass, he had only hung a few on and was, for him, slightly sober. Late at night it had to be the piano because standing to take a horn solo was often a problem. He was getting deeper in to the hunt for what it was on the other end of the secret door of jazz. And the piano chords rode up and down and somebody ran out to get another bottle of crack-skull. And the chippie he was dating hitched up her rolled stockings and said, 'Play it, Daddy.' There were a lot of cute pigeons always around and Bix liked the dames as much as the booze and the piano. Bix had manners, something they don't hand out to jazz players, and he looked clean-cut even when seedy, before he put on the fat. So the girls liked him. But the truth was, Bix was fixed on his mother in some way nobody ever tried to explain. She meant more to him than any of the girls."

Later Bix did a season at the Martinique in Indiana Harbor. "He played the horn like nobody and crowds came to hear him. He was the star of the Wolverines and everyone knew it. They didn't play much of a repertoire, mostly the old corny stuff that they made good in their own way. As they couldn't read music, except for two men, they didn't add much to their list of numbers. They played it over and over again for the people who liked it, maybe ten choruses of a number. They didn't appeal to the thousands of people who just want an excuse to dance to something, so in time they had to break up and look around on their own. It was the peak for the band, they had done their job. And for Bix—only he didn't know it—the beginning for him was over. He'd go higher before going lower, but it would never be the same as it had been in the early days—Bix taking it clear, good, just the way he wanted it, better and better."

In the novels they wrote about him, he was always looking for some new blue note and killing himself trying for it, tearing his heart out for it. But that wasn't it at all—and no girl drove him to it, and anyway there wasn't any girl, just girls. In that period when the band was still together he made music the way he wanted it. "He wasn't unhappy; he wasn't happy. He just drifted and played. There was home he could go to and he could still hold his likker and he wasn't fat yet: The music was still easy." It was the golden weather of his work and his time on earth. Only of course he didn't know it. He went to Chicago and got a job with Charlie Straight's orchestra.

"Bix didn't bother to read the orchestra score, just played by ear and read a wild-west novel he had open on his music-rack. Later, when almost everyone had gone home, Bix and the boys would blow it free and the jam was on. It was a job but he left when he found out the rest of the band was paying half his salary to keep him as their drawing-card. He began to hang out in the black-and-tan dives, the hot Negro places. Oliver and Louie, Bessie Smith he heard, and they sent him, really made him jump. Bix used to toss his salary on the floor to keep Bessie singing all night. He played in theaters and played wherever he could pick up a night's work, and he listened to Bessie give out with *I'll See You in My Dreams.* He forgot to eat, drinking shakeups and whatever booze the bootleggers were giving out with. He mixed with vipers on the reefer-trail, with studs shying a toy of opium. But there isn't much record that he went for tea-sticks or the smoke himself. Booze was enough.

"It was a tough go for real jazz players because the big sweet combos were coming in to cater to the tastes of the housewives and the office-help, dancing respectable as they could the Charleston and Lindy Hop, and even trying the Black Bottom and Big Apple. Bix played lake-boats and hung around spaginzy sessions jamming New Orleans style. He rattled around with the zooty mob and the yard-dogs sitting in dives and always he carried in his pocket the mouthpiece of

his cornet, taking it out and fingering it while he listened to others playing."

For a year, he played in Frank Trumbauer's band at the Arcadia Ballroom, St. Louie. "He was pulling down good money—a hundred bucks a week—but he never held on to it or spent it on himself. The rat's-nest of a crumb-bum hotel was enough, and running up stuff on the slate in the speaks. Three- or four-hundred-dollar tabs for unpaid likker. He didn't dress in the smart-set of threads as some jazzmen did; when he left town, he had on a borrowed pair of pants, and a friend's coat. His tuxedo trousers had gone shiny and given way in center-field, and so he never let the customers see him anything but front face.

"It was in St. Louie that he went daffy over modern music—the new concert stuff, new to him anyway: Ravel, Debussy, MacDowell and Stravinsky. The whole-tone scales and the whole-tone chords he was to work into his stuff came from here. He had a recording of *The Firebird Suite,* and he wore it out in no time.

"He spent more time on the piano, woodshedding and playing over and over again improvisations that built to new melodic content for him. Maybe he figured if he was a genius, this was the stuff that was going to make him come out true and real. But, meanwhile, there was a world outside of these new piano-chords. There was a job now out there, and a kind of fame. He went into Jean Goldkette's Orchestra, and the Indiana U College newspaper voted him in 1926 the greatest "dirty" trumpet-player in jazz circles. . . .' They put quotes around 'dirty' as if not sure just what the word meant.

"Goldkette's Band was a hot and sweet pop band and its main purpose was to make money. It did. It also indirectly made jazz respectable to a lot of people and sent others on their own to discover the real thing." The hot section that Bix played with was Trumbauer, Pee Wee Russell, Sonny Lee, Itzy Riskin and Ray Ludwig. They hit the Blue Lantern, at Hudson Lake, and Bix played cornet, piano and, a few times, the drums. But it was a high-priced band and when bookings got tough, Bix went over to Paul Whiteman. Whiteman was said to be worried over Bix as not being the kind of character that would fit into the sleek King of Jazz setup. But he took Bix on anyway. Paul Whiteman was a kind-hearted man and, while he may have muffed any idea of what jazz really was, he wasn't bad to work for. When Bix got sick, he took care of him and when Bix got the D.T.'s and the heebies set in, Whiteman treated Bix to a drunk cure.

"Bix played the sweet flash stuff, the modern concert music, but little by little, people came to stop and watch Bix go into a solo. Bix was getting fat now and there weren't many moments when he was feeling in key with the world. But he could still play the horn.

When the band played Los Angeles, Whiteman used Bix only in the hot group with Goldfield, Margulies and Busse.

"Back in Chicago, Bix used to start his night after the places closed and a dream-session would start with anybody who felt they could keep up with Bix—Freeman, the brothers Dorsey, Benny Pollack, Joe Sullivan—at white dives or Negro places in the South Side with just enough air to breathe, a piano and a place to stash the bottle. By this time, Bix was getting three-hundred a week and looking like a Loop hobo unless his friends tied his clothes on him properly.

"By 1929 Bix was on the way down—not yet on the skids, but the good time and the big time was behind him. He didn't like Whiteman's band any more. It was real commercial now and the radio dates were murder—the real classic corn. Radio meant twenty numbers in an hour, six of them usually new, and the tricky arrangements were sterile but tough for a man who was never much of a reader. The pressure, the tension, didn't help his frayed nerves and the whisky moved in for keeps. He was sick, everyone said. Not maudlin drunk, not jerky, just sick. After his cure, he went home to see the folks and explain to his mother some ideas he had.

"In 1931, he was out of Whiteman's band and picking up radio one-spots like the Camel Hour. Casa Loma wanted him but he could take only four nights of the exacting arrangements and tricky ensembles. He did a little recording with Tommy Dorsey, Joe Venuti, Eddie Lang, Bud Freeman, Bubber Miley, Gene Krupa and some others, and was his old self in part of the records.

"But it didn't hold for long. He was on the town. No dough in sight, he didn't really mooch, but it was a hard pickup every morning to go through the day." He was careless with things now, and himself most of all; the dream was going out of Bix, the wonder and awe of life, and he didn't seem to care. "If you didn't give a damn for him you said he was just a lush and anything happened to the bum, he asked for it. But if you knew him—he was still kind and full of charm and some place was the lost artist, mislaid, bricked up, buried away. What the hell can happen to a guy in a world where there isn't too much for the lug who wants to be different? The head-doctors can give it big words and speak of his family and how much he was still mother's boy. But they couldn't explain why there wasn't one lousy corner where he could have sat playing his kind of music, working out his own ideas of it. It might have been great, or it might have been nothing much. We'll never know now.

"One thing he got down on paper. He and Challis worked over three months on *In A Mist*. It was good, but you couldn't really say great. Bix had done it too close to the end. He was tired. He still played the piano for his friends and chiselers and hangers-on in his Forty-fourth Street hotel. That's about all he did. Play the piano and punish the whisky. He was always improvising on themes out of what he got from Debussy, and he sat there playing and it was all right. But it had no thread long enough to make something to play in a band and he didn't give a damn. He was on the wagon now, of course, and what he drank was with a wink and shake of the head. Everybody who knew Bix came to hear him, and Babe Ruth came, and a lot of horn and piano men who felt there was a little good stuff to lift here.

"Bix and his mother had talked it over, and what he was dreaming of was to tour Europe with some boys and show them the real white jazz. It needed backing and not too much at that. He had an audition, not with mugs, either, but the Dorseys, Krupa, Sullivan, Freeman. But the backing never came. He didn't care much after that. He didn't keep warm or well-fed. He got a bad cold and went out in a dismal night to blow his horn at a Princeton Club date. He knew they didn't want the band without Bix. So he went and let the college boys and their dates stare at him, sick and sweating, his head on fire and blocked off from air and the world. But he played.

"It came around to pneumonia and Bix tried to suck in air and he lay there and after a while went drifting." Nobody knows what sounds he heard. In the novels written about him, it was horn music, louder, better and rarer than any he had ever played before, or dreamed of. But that was literary corn. Most likely he just didn't care and inside his head, the horn was still. On August 7, 1931, he died. He was twenty-eight.

Go 'way from my window,
Quit scratchin' on my screen.
You're a dirty mistreater,
I know just what you mean.

Well, Mama she don't 'low me
To fool around all night long.
Now I may look like I'm crazy—
But I do know right from wrong.

DROP DOWN MAMA

Chapter 14

Bootlegger Blues

Alcohol and music in any normal mind are connected as something that often becomes a party. In the '20's there was a lot of alcohol and lot of music and it was hard later to take them apart and show that the music didn't bring in the likker, but rather that the booze gave a lot of the music a place to play and earn a living. "You can't understand what happened to jazz unless you remember what it was like in those days."

But a generation or so has come between us and the Awful Experiment, and it's almost forgotten—how it happened and how it worked and what it was like. Nobody reads anymore the novels they wrote about it—the movies of the period are wearing out, even on television—and nothing is as dead as an old newspaper headline.

But jazz was in the middle of it and furnished the theme song to the Great Drink. They made up words like scoff-law for it, and yet it's only the music of the period that brings it back to those who were there—"a small cellar-joint and fake grape-leaves on the ceiling and the dame crying in the phone booth, the smell of needled beer. And a blue piano."

The Jazz Age was toasted in bootleg booze. There was a demand for *drinking* alcohol in the land. If you drank it, you had only yourself to blame. The jazz bands played on. Violent activities and bright-eyed fortitude worked hand-in-hand. People were fermenting mash, cutting hair-tonic, recooking extracts: all gave gangsters, the local bootleggers an idea, and then an empire in the Jazz Age. They never puttered indecisively. They banged and took. Gangs spread out, contacted rum ships rolling on a leeshore twelve miles out. Jazz went to work in the speakeasies. Cargoes of whisky came ashore in the murky coves by fast cabin cruisers.

"The young polacks and micks quit their jobs in the packing plants and drove trucks guarded by imported mobsmen armed with Thompson submachine guns. The lads quit high school to pilot the beer-trucks; men organized ex-war buddies and hired out the boys when highjackers stopped cargoes at interurban boulevards. Some inventor put an electric-light bulb inside a banjo.

"Drugstore cowboys and bellhops degenerated to peddlers of booze. And this in simple American towns where the local sewer-graft, the stealing of school funds, had been normal, petty and in the American way. Jazz music was blamed for most of it. And jazz came into the home with the pocket-flask."

Jazz had grown up in Storyville; now, in the age of bootlegging, it grew into manhood—a full maturity.

Vice became smart; evil paid off as never before and the American cities roared and rattled in the grip of bootleg kings. Belly-laughs about gang killings, poisonings, hoods, tommyguns, speakeasies and jazzing flappers became commonplace.

Near-beer still within the law. Make all you want. Conjure it up by the legal barrel. First you make real beer, and then you take the alcohol out of it.

"Can anyone help it if the boys forget to take the alki out of most of the beer? Truckers come and haul it away. It's a laugh on the brewer—but a pleasant one, for they pay twice as much for this carelessly unfinished stuff as for the few crates or honest near-beer the brewer makes and sends out to the Negro jazz neighborhood where they needle it with ether. Boy, how that frog-beer gets you. Frog-beer? Sure, two glasses and you hop all the way home."

Hollywood discovered gangster movies—and every motion-picture had a jazz score, though not often with real jazz music. So the native hears lots of jazz, drinks his whisky, and in over the 19,000 miles of coastline and border the stuff pours into the American gullet. Just as crime becomes an everyday event in American homes, so jazz, too, moves from the dives, the slums, into respectable parlors.

Illicit distilling smokes up the hills and the far-off desert hovels, creeps underground into the mushroom cellars and cheerful Yankees, Wops, Negroes, give up bathing and set up a plant in their bathtubs. It's a living, pal. A five-hundred-dollar still will produce fifty to a hundred gallons of alcohol a day—and that's uncut. Steeped in duplicity, you split it with water, flavor, smoke, a few juniper berries, and you've a hundred to two hundred gallons of some apparently indispensable stuff. And a one-gallon portable still can be bought for six bucks.

The supply stores spring up. Make your own wine, brew your own beer, bottle your own apple, mule, King Kong, lightning, Panthersweat, and may God have mercy on your liver.

The roaring mandate is *drink it down! Chicago, Chicago—that wide-open town.*

Drink, brew, distill. Truck, kill and highjack. Smear, bribe and beat, Charleston and ball-the-jack. Say hello, Judge; palm over a fistful of long green to the agents. Smile at the Coast Guards, the Custom Service—their hearts ain't in it. An agent is a sap to toil and get his guts shot out of him for two grand a year, to take the initiative against an army. Not with Santa Claus around to hand out candy.

Andy Volstead, making America rich, giving work to boys who have mothers and broads to support, making drinking fun, renting old brownstone houses and bringing in New Orleans and Dixieland and Chicago and Harlem jazz. Printing cards for Social Clubs, making friends and feeding jazz players. *"Joe sent me." "Remember me? I was here last night."*

And out on the heaving pond among the spindrift and the spume, the rum-ships stand out to sea from Bimini, Belize, St. Pierre, the cargoes come in speed-boats from Detroit, go in launches up the old Canal, drift across the Canadian border, are hoisted in on freights, with manipulation of seals, passed by alcohol cookers and crime rings. The jazzmen had jobs again, amusing the new rich.

It was amazing how nothing changed on the surface and how everything slowly became colored and stained by the flood of crime, with jazz music as its sound effects.

"People got used to finding a slug-eaten body in a ditch. They rolled their heads and said: 'Them bootleggers,' and went home to try out the home-brewed beer made of raisins and yeast and to think profoundly of setting up a speakeasy. They wound up the Victrola and played *Hot Five* records. Drink. Drink it down.

"Warrants, legal papers, postponements—a little smearing of the right palm? Let the lawyers do it. All liquor cases accepted with alacrity. Want to buy sugar, medical alcohol, copper stills, real honest-to-God protection? Have Mr. Big give you the introduction to a cordial lawyer. Pay your money and don't ask questions. None of your business what judges get their cut, what Federal Agent buys a new car. Have you heard Bix play on his cornet?

"The town's druggists are selling jazz records now as well as booze. Doing fine, too. Doctors will give you a drug-store prescription—for a fee—give you a book of them if you want them. Sure your cold is worse; sure, you need a prescription. Nothing like a good hot cup of tea and a case of Haig and Haig whiskey."

The Feds can't even stop 5 per cent of it. The trucks pound along in the night hours, pass through, loaded high, go skipping across the bridge, keep coming—even from U. S. Warehouses—at the rate of fifteen-million gallons a year. If you know the State Boss, he knows the people who hand out the warehouse permits. And one gallon of

alcohol cut three times, with fresh labels lying their heads off, is sold as *"just off the boat."* Jazz-band joke: "Yeah—scraped right off the bottom."

Hip-pockets in every new suit. Give a pocket-flask for a birthday gift. The jazz flappers and the sax-playing boy friends all drink. Every football game has its scores of drunks. Over ten-thousand bottles were removed after one Yale-Harvard game.

"Joe College wears a racoon and collects Louie Armstrong records. The Sicilians have opened cellar-dives, the cops get their free snort, the patrons pay, everybody drinks in squalid rookeries full of barrelhouse piano. The gals wear dresses cut above their knees, their nude thighs are pink, their stockings rolled as they Black Bottom and Lindy Hop. Even the girls at high-school have stopped wearing underwear and buy Red Nichols numbers by the dozen.

"Travelling salesmen carry their own stuff, all deals made in hotel bedrooms are final—ice and ginger-ale on the bill. Bellhops are cleaning up and buying clarinets to copy King Oliver's style."

Izzy Einstein and Moe Smith carry on a fast raid, have six places padlocked. Next week—business as usual. Virgins, reporters, housewives, kept-wenches, customer's men hunt the brass rail and keep the radio on that Cab Calloway *Minnie the Moocher.* The newspapers make hay. Crime waves, immorality, divorce rates increase. Every hovel, every shack has a still and a radio and jazz records. Mama makes it, papa bottles, the kids peddle it and learn the ropes. Nellie goes into a house to meet the bug buyers, Buddy drives for Capone or Dutch to learn the routes—and there are enough customers for all the small fry. The jazz bands can't turn it out fast enough. Tin Pan Alley fakes the jazz—the sweet swing is no longer the real stuff. Razzmatazz takes over. Agents appear to exploit the jazz players, to take big cuts of their take. Jazz booking becomes a racket.

Gangland takes over the building trades, the bus lines, the jazz joints. The big businessmen hold meetings, talk, over good cigars. What to do? The cops are all working for Al or Joe, the law-and-order boys are on mob payrolls. And their guns are tough and handy and have no respect for names—old American families. They were good boys in their day when we could handle them.

There are guns for hire. One hundred dollars for a black-powder bomb, one-thousand for a dynamite job, fifty bucks to break an arm. A hundred will break two legs, a shellacking costs five hundred—but lays the victim up for six months. A rub-out is a thousand —a complete job with a big black car and three hoods with a tommy-gun, two-thousand. A trifle for a good job. A jazz-club comic gets knifed.

"That's how jazz came in with an era of crime, and that's how jazz got a bad name. It didn't do anything but play the music that made the twenties roar—but it took a long time before people forgot all the crime with its background of jazz music."

The boys who meet on Randolph Street
An art-forsaken mob,
Do not talk Bix or fancy licks—
They're praying for a job . . .

RANDOLPH STREET

Chapter 15

A Style Called Chicago

There are places in New York or New Orleans or Chicago where the unemployed jazz players hang out, their heads pushed into upturned coat-collars, their horns in a battered case, their neckties daring, and their tailoring sharp but worn. They stand in the sun and talk about the old days and the old music. They eat hastily and not much in the little tired places where the food is cheap and the coffee can be sat over for a long time. They come out chewing a free toothpick, the hunger still on them. They ask for a gig in some roadhouse, maybe how to pick up a spot on radio or tear off a recording for some fly-by-night company. Or just stand and wait. These are the men who make jazz. There are never enough jobs and too many new kids who think all you have to do is make music and the world is waiting for the sunrise of your talents, like the Tin Pan Alley tunes tell you.

"Chicago style came out of a lot of this standing around, of kids and old-timers talking it over and trying it on. It was a school and a style, and should be judged for what it did best and not for what it didn't do, and often didn't try to do."

The Chicago school didn't come from Bix alone. It came from a stronger mixture of Dixieland and King Oliver and Louie. From

1927 to 1930 (and this dating is not too accurate, no matter what the form-books say) Chicago school, or style, was a mixture of both. Muggsy Spanier and the *Bucktown Five* did some good things in it and recorded their best in *Mobile Blues, Everybody Loves My Baby,* and others. The tempo is very fast, but the feel of the rhythmic beat is fine.

By 1930, ahead of our story, the *Rhythm Kings* disbanded and pure Dixieland left Chicago. Chicago style pretty much held the field. Louie Armstrong was still recording classical jazz with the Armstrong *Hot Five, New Orleans Bootblacks* and the *New Orleans Wonders.* Jelly Roll Morton was recording his *Red Hot Peppers,* so jazz wasn't really dying as the lamenters and chest-beaters claimed.

Chicago style was true to jazz and goes back to 1922 (you have to backtrack a lot and pick up clues where you can in jazz—it has no official historians). "Five punks at Chicago's Austin High School got up a band of sorts. They were Bud Freeman, Frank Teschemacher, Jim Lannigan, Jimmy and Dick McPartland. They drifted into *The Wolverine* group and Dick McPartland replaced Bix who had fallen apart and was on the sauce most of the time. In 1927 they began recording the first of the Chicago style."

Moving away from the usual rhythmic jazz beat, they did *China Boy, Nobody's Sweetheart, Bull-Frog Blues* and others. "They used a heavy beat and it gets kind of hot and high. Chicago style had a trade mark—breaking its beat up into successive patterns. They used the riff in their own way—not as what it has since become in swing. Maybe the solos are showoff but they are good Chicago style. The harmonized sections are arranged and the technical facility is amazing. Any statement that it always shows lack of real creativeness is nonsense." Teschemacher's clarinet is wildly rhapsodic and is played out of tune in dissonance and quarter-tones. This is modern to some, and shocking to others. Tesch played free-for-all and certainly not New Orleans style. Chicago style tried to develop into a modern music. ("It must be admitted it hasn't gone far, but there is nothing to prevent a genius appearing and taking Chicago Style into true jazz greatness.")

Whatever it did, Chicago style moved on. Wingy Manone, Sid Catlett and Frank Melrose played it. Pee Wee Russell took over when Teschemacher was killed in an auto accident. Pee Wee's spit and growl tones drove the purists into a frenzy of condemning remarks. The later Chicago style can best be studied in such sides as *Sugar, Barrel House Stomp,* and *Tillie's Downtown.* A fine barrel-house piano player, George Zack, helped. All in all, it was a good attempt to show that all white jazz is not just an off-shoot of Dixieland, copied note for note.

Oh, Sister, Ain't it Hot shows Chicago style leading into public jam-sessions. The original sitting-in stuff had been a collection of serious jazzmen taking it over and trying it out, but the public jam-sessions were exhibits of wild bouts of sound.

"The worst you could say about it was that it was fun, maybe, but not profound. Like everything else, jam-sessions weren't always what they claimed to have been when they first appeared and took on showman values. Let's not bury Chicago style. It didn't commit all the errors in instrumentation, in tone, rhythm, phrasing and ensemble it was blamed for. It was true to Chicago; it fitted the town; it played earnestly the way it felt; and all it lacked were a few geniuses of jazz to make it shine and make it show what it could do. . . ."

All you gals get out and walk
'Cause he's gonna start his dirty talk . . .
BLUE PIANO

Chapter 16

The Ivory Floor

The piano came late to jazz, drifted in, stayed around and made for itself a place and a way of playing the blues. Playing them ragtime, playing them barrelhouse, boogie-woogie, and if you admitted or admired the stuff, playing them swing.

"They gave a lot of reasons for a blue piano. Fancy ones about a lonely man and soul lost in memory; about a lost past, and a lot of high-class corn like that. But the piano player played the blues mostly because there was a buck in it—a chance to mooch a drink, to play for his friends, to try out a new stuff crawling around in his brain and at the ends of his fingers.

"They never played hot piano before the blues and when at last the Negro got to a piano, he disregarded its limitations. In fact, he never heard of them. No matter what they called it, it was black playing on the white ivory floor of the keyboard. Up until 1900 there had been a few barrelhouse players knocking it off among the kegs of corn-whisky, and all they left were their names—Old Florida Sam, Bricky Johnny, Trigger Sam, Skinny-Head Pete, and a few you couldn't repeat in polite society. The ragtime boys had more class, even some of that stuff called sophistication. Al Cahill, Al Wilson, Sam Davis: they played it, let's face it, as whorehouse music. And some, like Jelly Roll and Tony Jackson, could sing with it. Blue piano, hot piano, you might as well call it jazz piano even if it *isn't* admitted to be just like a group with horns and string-bass and a set of traps. The jazz boys worked without the piano at first, and it isn't essential to a jazz band. But it helps, and on its own it's a good sound to hear."

The first blue piano players were just mugs that drifted around playing guitar, most likely, when there was no piano. "He hit it solid and with no nonsense, transposing the chord and the rhythm, the pattern the way it felt in his head. It wasn't a voice to him, it was a drum." Barrelhouse was primitive, archaic, but real. It touched ragtime, it was stomp and it was solid blue. Boogie-woogie, when it came along later and found a name, was a special kind of blue piano. But don't think of it on a concert grand, an acre of Steinway teak or rosewood.

"How do you make a blue piano? Find a saloon or a madame that owns a battered upright. Be sure it's old and loose in action. And if its in tune, beat it a bit until it takes on that special out-of-tune twang, because the bright boys will call that jazz dissonance on the blue scale. Pick a crate with a so-called mandolin attachment, so that when the plucked note is right you get yourself almost a harpsichord, whatever the hell that was. And don't make it sound too clean. The old dirty tone is best for barrelhouse blues. To get it, pad the piano strings with old newspapers or some burlap bag and kick the front board, hit it hard for drum rhythm. Don't care how it looks, but pay attention how it sounds. They don't make pianos like that anymore. Only the best junkyards have a few prime ones left.

"And don't ever try to play barrelhouse on concert grands. That's for the guy with the long hair on his head, in a monkey-suit on a stool. Guzzleshop piano is the only kind to grind out *Barrelhouse Woman, Shreveport Farewell* and the *Harry Brown Blues.* Keep that treble tremolandi on the ground bass, and end in the descending bass." The slow blues need it, that walking bass going up and coming down the spread octaves, and the delayed beat of a breathing locomotive. Blue piano with broken treble chords and talkin' blues is the real barrelhouse. One of the best was Cripple Clarence Lofton. They call him bawdy and archaic now.

Woke up this mornin' feelin' bad
Thinkin' about times I've had.
You went out and stayed all night—
Do you think that's treatin' me right?

Oh, you shouldn't do it at all
Shouldn't do it at all . . .

I'm tellin' you lover
How do you strut that thing
Night and day . . .

Gettin' sick and tired of the way you do
God, Mama, gonna pizon you.
Sprinkle goofer dust on your bed—
Wake up some mornin'
Find yourself dead . . .

Spreckled Red (also called Rufus Perryman) was rough but good. He did *You Got To Fix It, The Dirty Dozens, Welfare Blues* and *St. Louis Stomp.* Red hit a strong percussion, twangy and noisy. He used the high treble keys and did a fine job on the string arpeggios.

Barrelhouse piano wasn't all black. George Zack's ghost walks over the recordings of *Muggsy Spanier's Ragtime Band.* Kansas City Frank Melrose did a fine *Pass The Jug* and he bowed to a good man in his *Jelly Roll Stomp.* Art Hodes produced a mean barrelhouse in *South Side Shuffle* and *Ross Tavern Boogie.* What the boys recorded remains—but a million great jobs are lost, forgotten long ago except by men growing older, if no wiser, and remembering the old bars and houses and the battered uprights. Men like Don Elwell carry on in *Buddy Bolden Blues, Manhattan Stomp,* and *Albert's Blues.*

The true barrelhouse is always percussion. "You attack the keys and with the sounding-board and sustained pedal the twang is extended. Boogie-woogie is really treble variations over a rhythmic stirring in the bass, making the most of rising and falling chords. The right hand improvises jazz variations and the left gives the rhythmic pattern to the rising and falling figures. Boogie piano isn't easy; it's serious and takes time. Boogie comes from the roots of banjo and guitar-playing and it reached high heaven around Kansas City, Chicago and St. Louie, by way of Texas and Alabama and other states south. It wasn't called boogie, not until around 1928, when a song called *Pine Top's Boogie Woogie* was recorded.

"Then depression came and the horns were in hock. You could always wrassel up a piano and get together to listen and charge a few coins and have a skiffle. Or, as some said, a rent party, or a shake, or a percolator. But whatever it was called it had a boogie piano and maybe a few cats, and the money paid the rent and the corner store and a little gin. Everybody got primed and everybody got gay and the arm-breakers rolled from the piano keys until the cops busted in or the host tossed you out in the crayon-blue of morning. Those were cold days, Mr. Hoover.

"Maybe the first real great boogie-woogie player was Jimmy Yancey. He had it—technique, fingers and a mind that invented things: *The Fives, Midnight Stomp, The Yancey Stomp.* He had a fancy bass, just right, and the right kind of smoky locomotive rhythm." There was a lot of good piano music around then: *Bugle Call, Low-Down Bugle Rag, Alley Drag, Four-Day Blues.* Pine Top Smith cut some of the first sides of boogie piano. "He would have done better, only he got in between on a dance floor and somebody's bullet cut him down. They never found out if it was meant for him. But he made some of the best piano music—*They Can't Do That, Jump Steady Blues, Now I Ain't Got Nothin' at All, Pine Top Blues.* How he made the old train run and the upright shake."

Meade Lux Lewis was another top hand and he recorded for Solo Art, Blue Note, English Parlophone, Victor and Paramount.

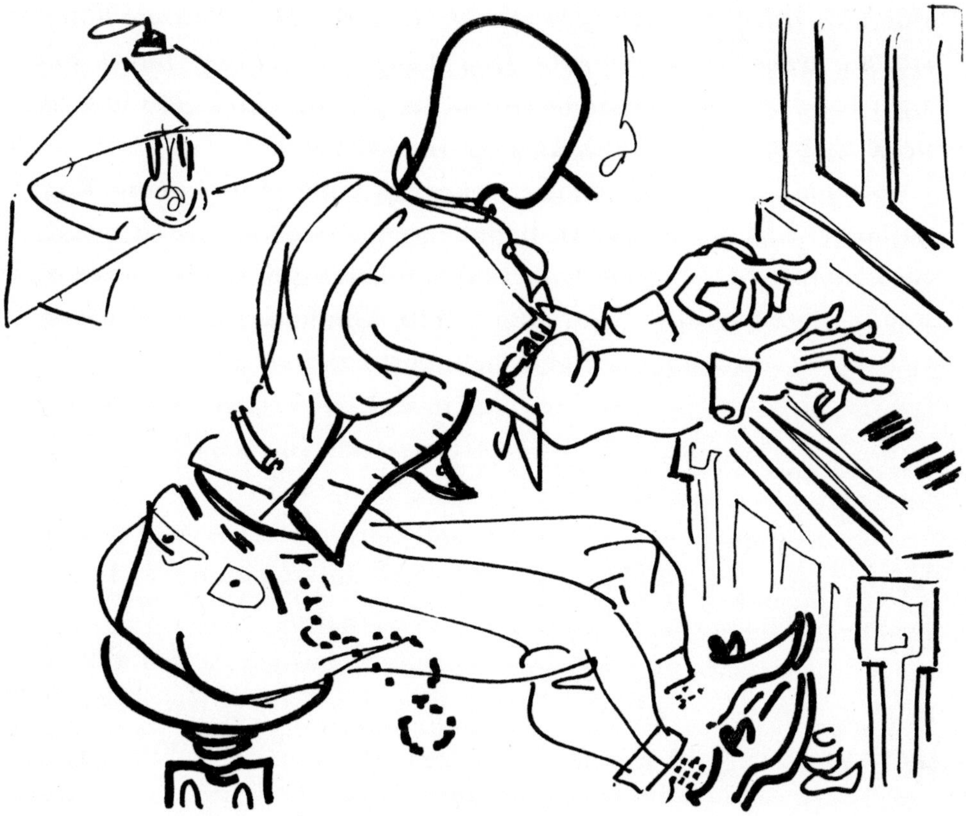

"Some say you can't overrate boogie-woogie; some claim it's just a cult, just a *tour de force.* In good hands it's among the best, and Lewis did it right in *Traveling Blues* and *Honky Tonk Train Blues.* There were a lot of good ones. Classics now. *Cow Cow Blues, I Had a Dream, South End Boogie, In The Mornin'.* But Meade Lux Lewis remained among the best. No one has done better than *Six Wheel Chaser, Deep Fives, Bear Cat Crawl, Whistlin' Blues* and *Celeste Blues.* And for the uptown critics, he rocked them back on their heels with a four-part improvisation with a Carnegie Hall title, *Variations on a Theme.*

"There was Albert Ammons, Pete Johnson, Jabbo Williams and lots of others. They made *Shout for Joy, Mecca Flat Blues, Buss*

Robinson Blues, Kaycee On My Mind, Head-Rag Hop, Suitcase Blues, Hasting Street, Roll 'Em Pete, How Long—How Long? But names don't help much. You have to hear it. Sit around with a glass in your hand and a drag smoking on your lip, and just listen."

Ragtime always held up through all kinds of new piano. Ragtime was good and it stayed. It was raggy, rhythmic, double-timed, always full of fun. The left hand played it in octaves, single or chords, and mostly did the 4/4 over into 2/4. The right hand took the melody in a free way. Running ahead or behind the melody added to the variety. Ragtime piano was the big stuff in St. Louie—from 1896 to 1917 on any street somebody was always trying it out. In 1904 they had ragtime contests at the *Meet Me in St. Louie, Louie* Fair.

"Nothing stays as it is or was, and ragtime was too good to keep out the money boys, Tin Pan Alley, the fake and imitation rags. Irving Berlin did a lot of this. He used it but added nothing new to it.

"It was easy to like ragtime piano. It was gay, it had a drive to it, and worth watching; left hand moving fast, so fast no fancy character trained to play the long-hair stuff could ever even come near how it combined rhythm with the right hand.

"Meade Lux Lewis was about the best, but Lucky Roberts was up there. Lucky got to New York around 1900 and did early rags like *Junk Man, Ragtime King, Shy and Sly, Ripples On The Nile.* He began the Harlem piano school, the shouts (a special kind of northern piece). Lucky had the fastest right hand on record, and even his pupil, James P. Johnson, couldn't play at his speed.

"When ragtime fell off it was still good, but not what it once was. There is a letdown in *Mah Jong* and *Panther Rag.* Earl 'Father' Hines was active in this period. The growth of the sophisticated Harlem piano did damage. They had odd names, the first Harlem boys—Kid Lippy, the Beetle, Jack the Bear . . . It wasn't too bad. Something new—real new—was the style that was a mocking copy of the paper piano-roll. It took over from the long paper roll the tremolando and the two-handed dropping breaks, just the way the rolls did them. Harlem style piano features all this.

"James P. Johnson was a great man on the rolls. Till 1920 he punched a lot of rolls. After that, he recorded sides. He was a blue cluster player: making the minor and major thirds and sevenths stick together. *Keep Off the Grass* and *Carolina Shout* show him at his best before he sluffed off. His pupil, Thomas 'Fats' Waller, was a character —a solid player. At a time when jazz was taking a beating from pop bands, he managed mostly to stay one of the real good jazz piano players. He did *Muscle Shoal Blues, Birmingham Blues, Ain't Misbehavin', I've Got A Feeling, Numb Fumbling, Smashing Thirds, Clothes Line Ballet, You're Not The Only Oyster In The Stew. . .* Fats liked life, sauce and fun."

The piano came into the band and stayed there, but a lot of the old New Orleans jazz never got around to piano parts. "The blue piano in the band under the fingers of men like Jelly Roll or Fats was in keeping with the band tempo. It didn't stand up and shout by itself. It had its place and kept it. It was a sort of transmission belt between the rhythm and the melody. They merged each other's beat and kept off the treble. The solos were there, but to carry the music forward, not to take hand-stands." Jelly Roll is tops on such recordings as *Freakish, Fat Meat and Greens, Mister Joe* and *Creepy Feeling.*

Alex Hill, Mary Lou Williams, Joe Sullivan, Jess Stacy, Art Tatum and Teddy Wilson all played blue piano and in their styling we can see the good solid stuff declining somewhat into fancy decorations; exhibitionistic manners taking over until with Earl Hines the piano almost becomes vaudeville.

"However, they were all able, all earnest. Yet modern piano has hit the slides, become decadent in form and method. Maybe it was the fact that no great creative talent came along who could play it clean of the pseudo-blue, the fake boogie-woogie, the Tin Pan Alley ragtime. Bix tried, and Debussy and Delius got into the woodpile, and yet that wasn't a crime. Good music is made up of many parts. But there wasn't anyone big enough to dominate the popularization and the impressionists and make it better than ever. Duke Ellington tried to make modern piano blues into an art-form as high as New Orleans and Dixieland. Jelly Roll Morton came closest.

"Barrelhouse remains today a good thing and a blue thing, a place for a man to sit and take down his emotions and let the blues drip off his fingers. Tomorrow or tomorrow or tomorrow, some kid will come along and show us how great it really is."

The old piano player knows it's old-fashioned to think the piano has a soul. To him the piano is often a woman—girlhood. She never finds, he feels, full satisfaction in life or love; mixed, crossed as she is, she can never forget her own tragic individuality or accept another. The piano remains in part the upper middleclass bourgeois, the scapegoat for sins she never fully knew she committed. She moves across life, baffled by chance and the configurations of mixed motives—going from austerity to availability—like a filing of steel to a magnet. The process of early aging is sudden and painful to the blue piano. She grows old suddenly, not at all gracefully or gradually. She grew, in the eyes of society anyway, evil, unmoral, with no effort on her part to know it or stop it.

The old piano player senses she feels the world's preoccupation with war and death and violence. She is colored by some of the recurrent nihilism of the times; perhaps because of it she is able to turn the edges of personal dramatic tension inward and harm herself. The piano is an odd tragic trinity in herself: the object, the sound and the search. Her tragedy reaches its climax for all the exertions and sacrifices of her decency, her breeding, her romantic nature, in a splitting-up of her life into a long-lost brooding childhood, and into a debauch of her wire nerve-ends. She is like those medieval saints who perverted their godhead by licking the sores of lepers and eating dung for the greater glory of some vague half-understood defilement. *Or maybe the old piano player is drunk and thinking too much.*

There is in the piano the disembodied will or what has been called the sterile will. The other will, the human will, is missing. The jazz piano is like something inherited from a romantic past that never fully made its mind up. *The old piano player needs another drink.*

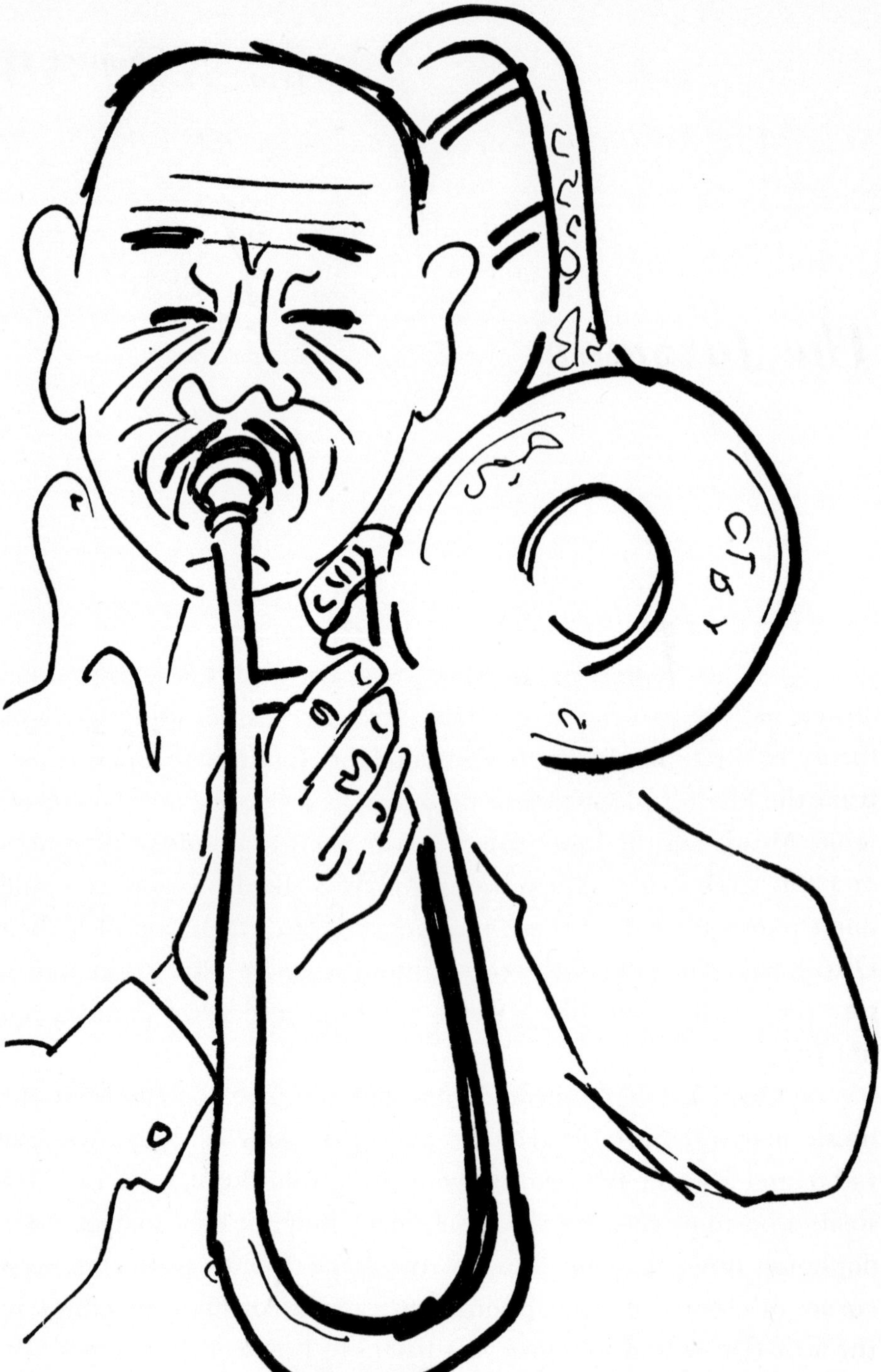

Comin' through the Palisades I lost my way,
Thought I was back on the road
Workin' for MCA . . .

TEAGARDEN BLUES

Chapter 17

The Jazzman

There is no school to learn jazz. There are no endowed halls where the bright boys are sent to study the history or theory of the thing. It's more than a talent: It's an urge and it comes from the kind of places where the music is good, but not too respectable. Mostly it's the lower side of town, the wrong side of the tracks or palm trees that produce the jazz-players. Bankers' sons as a rule don't play jazz, even if there was Roger Wolfe Kahn, son of banker Otto Kahn who gave, they said, millions to opera. But Roger was so rare they treated him like a freak, and he played sweet ragtime, not hot jazz.

"So a kid looks around him and life isn't too easy, but the music makes it bearable. He listens to the music in dives, over the radio, and a whole new world opens up to him through his ears. He steals a horn, or gets one cheap in a hock-shop, he cons someone in a flophouse mission to let him use the come-to-Jesus piano, he plays cornet or clarinet in some phony charity band, or finds something in the attic that will make music. He listens to Louie or the jazz hounds' records, he copies, he tries, he plays around. He finds some other kids as crazy as he is about the music and they compare notes and blow chords and set up a small combine and play for peanuts at dances. And try to get a steady job. The misery starts.

"There's an old cornball of a story in the school-books about the king who sent out his wise men to put down all the knowledge of the world, and when they came back with huge volumes of it, he sent them back again and again to cut it down—until years later they had it all down to one small book. Maybe if they had worked on it longer they would come up with the whole story in a line from a blues-song not written yet: We are born in a dream and die in dust."

You could collect thousands of records and play all the sides ever made to get a history of jazz, or you could just pick up a dozen or so numbers and you'd have the whole story. A few players of the music are maybe saying the same thing with their blue notes: "You are born in a dream and die in dust."

"Jazz music, right back to the archaic, was the music of some friends in sympathy, music-makers in cooperation. It goes about like this when you make jazz: a guy, a couple or a trio, five or seven, sit down to make it all over. To create music together. Not fighting each other, all pulling for the main end. The horn takes a theme. The clarinet pulls an intricate polyphony around it. Someone takes over the harmony for a minute—somebody imitates and drifts off into rhythmic phrases. It grows in each man, it is the whole and the everything of what he feels, what his personal chemistry is in brain and gut and bowel and heart. And it's something remembered, something added, something new. You add a little counterpoint of percussion and exhibit a little of the harmonic progress. They come together, they separate from you as individuals. But they never go too far. You play for yourself, but in key with everybody else the phrasing is overall. You keep it rolling, never let the ball stop rolling, you jog it along with little breaks and runs. You play the way the horn plays; the traps are needed and the string-bass is back there overseeing the background. Now you really let it out—a free improvised singing inside you, coming out in brass or wood or hide. It's coherent, logical and what they call a variation on a theme. And when it's just right and everyone is feeling hep, why you can even go into a variation *inside* a variation. You free-wheel but you're under control, and man, it's smooth, and the solo steps out and blows it and you chime along and follow his climb. Every phrase fresh, free, clear—the hell with the clichés of the pop bands. You start with the score, but from then on you're on your own. Something you'll never do the same way again no matter how you play that number. It can't be, they say, that a group of characters in a session become one single unit making something good, but it happens. Everybody is a solid swinging gate and you're no longer a pickup band—you don't see the mike any more or worry about the turntable cutting the side. You're making music, and if you spoil this side, you'll do the next one better and bigger and wider and stronger."

So there are thousands of records, but only a fistful of guys really made the classics. King Oliver, Jelly Roll Morton, Louis Armstrong, George Michell, Kid Grey, Honore Dutrey, Johnny Dodds, Omer Simeon, Johnny St. Cyr. A handful of others, fill in your own names.

There's a moving unity about good records like *Bull Fiddle Blues, Weary City Stomp, Perdido Street Blues,* and *Too Tight Papa* that these men did.

"Louie has done almost six-hundred sides in his time, maybe more by now. With Oliver, Tate, Henderson and lots of others. He's a real jim-dandy virtuoso, complex yet clear. Full of fun, full of mood and able to take a whole chorus on a single high note." His glissando is amazing and yet so simple it lives in everything he tried. "Alone, he's a great man. Sometimes with the bands he lets down his quality of what he does and he's done pop and radio and TV just a little below the dignity of such a great horn. But a good man can be permitted a lot of things. He went into swing, and if you like it or not he brought over to it two good things: a hot accent and solid timbres." The big bands were made for swing and they pulled Louie along.

"Some say he let jazz down, that he went into something too complex for the early New Orleans stuff, that he was in danger of going like Duke Ellington after a mixture of concert swing and fashionable European modern. But, really, there has never been a sign of that in Louis Armstrong. He stands alone, yet part of what he was and came from. A creator and a jazz individualist. Maybe he's left the groups that best served him. But there has never been any progress made by groups. It was always some daring, some splendid guy with a new idea who broke all the rules, invented all the big changes; in writing books, making shoes, painting pictures, starting a new country *or* playing jazz."

"They all had it: Buddy Bolden, Oliver, Morton, Armstrong; the understanding that the ivory tower was a hell of a good way of identifying yourself with the tomb. They went out among people and made mistakes and got better. They learned the hard way between the easy beauty of things, which is soft, agreeable and pleasing, and the sublime, which is full of the sentiments of fear, the infinite, and hard times and sad times. Maybe they couldn't say it with words, long words, but the short shout did just as well. The jazzmen weren't cunning, not the way Lord Bacon said it: 'Cunning is crooked wisdom. Nothing is more hurtful than when cunning men pass for wise.' Tin Pan Alley, the pop bands, are cunning. . . . The jazz boys playing it their own way, somehow, in looking back, they seem wise. *Not* practical about food, likker, women, shelter, no, not practical—*just* wise."

They don't talk about it much in writing; they don't spout the long phrases explaining what it is they're doing or how. They've learned to be almost mystic about jazz because scientific and philosophical intentions of people remain merely intentions. "Creating anything real and good hasn't been perfectly charted or explained yet.

Sometimes they fight among themselves for the wrong reason, and like a weak dame, they end by being right by the sheer shouting of being wrong. But they don't fool themselves for long."

They don't read Stendhal: "The passionate man does not laugh." Watch the solid jazzmen sometimes when the passion is on them and they bend over the tools of music and turn it on. "The public laugh is gone, the yak-yak is put away, the big ropey dark laughter of other moments just isn't there. Music is dead serious stuff when it reaches the crest and you want to go up and over it without falling down.

"We all fall short of the results we might have achieved. The jazz player never reaches full maturity of his art. *That* is always there before him; he runs toward it, reaches for it, and one more—the next step—he will have it. . . . So he plays, the years pass, the misery and the ache stays—and always just the next step, just out of reach of his fingertips—that's where it will always remain."

"Sometimes they say jazz reached maturity between 1924 and 1928 and that everything since is down-grade. But that isn't true; it was very good then but when the next wave hits high and lifts its crest again it will go even bigger and better. For there is no absolute in jazz; just as there isn't in any art-form any more. You think it's the absolute, but it's only yesterday's pale sunlight. . . .

"Jazz is a language but horns don't really talk. You have to change the words into tones, and jazz is close to Chinese forms, a rhythmic tonal idiom special in itself like Balinese gong-music or Japanese *gaga-ku.* It beats out tough music for hard dancing in the black-and-tan joints, but it's not just dance music, as many think. It's tonal coloration. It's a lot more. It's in a way a cross-fertilization between the real blues and men like Bartok, Copland, Krenek, Harris and Thompson trying on the new in concert music. Stravinsky's *Petrouchka* or Ravel's *Rhapsodie Espagnole* may show jazz effects, but they are not jazz. Concert or traditional music lets the accent of the rhythm fall on the beat; they may try syncopation, which is the shifting or moving of the regular metrical accent, but that doesn't make them true jazz. Ragtime goes a little way toward jazz as it makes the principle of continuously suspended rhythm, but it was not true jazz either—just a signpost in the right direction."

Ragtime first appeared in 1896 as a word on the sheet-music used by Bert Williams, the Negro comic, on his song *Oh, I Don't Know, You're Not So Warm.* Ragtime had ease and fluidity and rhythmic suspensions. It could be written down. A lot of jazz can't be notated—at least, according to some schools. Folk esthetes make a lot of rules that cause trouble. Real art breaks all rules.

The Negro made his own music fit the personal needs of baptism and burial singing. It explained his brooding ideas of trouble.

If your house catches fire
An' they ain't no water 'round
Throw your trunk out de window
An' let the shack burn down.

It's a way of looking at life that doesn't expect the beautiful or the perfect.

Oh, I love to hear my baby
Call my name.
She can call it so easy
An' so dog-gone plain.

"The colored fiddlers and banjo players did it up before the horn and the piano came around for jigs, reels, cotillions and contradances. The mandolin, guitar and string-bass helped, and when that was missing, the pebble-filled gourd, the half-cask viol did as well. Cutting contests caught on—those tests in improvisation." The early jazzman said plain, when he wanted. He couldn't read music. And those that did were rare, and often said "I can read music-notes, but I *can't* separate 'em."

"Jazz was called a lot of things and twisted to form new ones: jabo, jaba, jazpation, jazynco, jazorient, jazanola, almost anything start-

ing in jazz. Jazanata, jazarella, jazanjaz, but it remained good jazz or poor. Jazology, jazette, jazitis and jazioso." It wasn't the spelling that counted; it was what it said.

No, I ain't rough
An' I don't fight,
But the woman that gits me
Got to treat me right . . .

And sometimes what being treated right meant was a pretty simple thing:

Cause I'm crazy about my lovin'
Must have it all the time.
It takes a brown-skin woman
To satisfy my mind . . .

"It didn't remain that simple or that pure. Popular songs were arranged as jazz and the music was good jazz if it was played right. The trumpet just went along inventing middle register solos and the blue singers tried it on. Mammie Smith, Clara Smith, Butterbeans and Susie, Maggie Jones, Lillie Delk Christian, Malissa Nix, and, of course, Bessie Smith—the best of all the Smiths. It was free-wheeling. You could make a stomp out of *Nagasaki,* do trumpet piano with *Tight Like This* or get mixed oral effects into Fats Waller's *Honeysuckle Rose.* Only don't be impressed because Fats was the only jazzman to ever play the organ of Notre Dame de Paris.

"You could play it real, could earn a buck in the pop bands or take an ad in *Billboard* and say you played it and 'read, fake, plenty hot.' Benny Goodman could talk about the Budapest Quartet and Joseph Szigetti sitting in, or the drummer could be smoking the dried leaves of the Indian hemp plant *cannabis indica* . . . it was all fun unless a Joe Below was cutting union scale.

"Maybe the scufflers who did one-night stands were derelicts and lushes. But they often played it purest. Sweet Sue in B-Flat with ten choruses. It sounds just as good then and you can get a tab on the bar, or can write it off on the slate."

Some people call me a hobo
Some people call me a bum.
Nobody knows my name,
Nobody knows what I've done.
I'm as good as any woman in your town.
I'm no high yella
I'm a deep yella-brown.
I ain't gonna marry,
Ain't gonna settle down . . .

When it's best, the music is clear and simple, easy to do (or looks as if it's easy), and it's direct and says it right out:

Easy rider struck this burg today
On a south-bound rattler
Side-door Pullman car.
Seen him here and he was on the hog—
Easy rider got to stay away . . .

Billie Holiday was the new kind of blues singer. "The older gals were gone or stashed away, the blue-music had to change a bit and go places a little smarter—but not better. Billie could sing it and make it feel like trouble because Billie was often in trouble herself:

Love, love, love, makes you walk on air.
Somebody touch you on the shoulder,
You turn around
There ain't nobody there.

Dreamed about a reefer five foot long
The mighty mezz, but not too strong;
You'll be high, but not for long
If you're a viper . . .

IF YOU'RE A VIPER

Chapter 18

Vices and Words

Jazz is close to the idea that man is the victim of his code of conduct and his unattainable ideals—and not (in the European view) of a blind struggle against fate.

"The pleasures of the jazzman are few. They are not hard to get. And most of them are not respectable." He doesn't collect first editions, or Braque. He doesn't walk in the country for his health or color a pipe or breed roses. "Once in a while a bandleader will race speedboats or collect pistols, but the jazz-player on his time off grabs what he can, and uses it the way it comes." Like the saint, he is aware we are born *inter urinas et faeces.*

Usually there are no roots; he sometimes gets a letter, badly spelled, a long way from home. "He lives in a hired room with a bottle for company and a pack of reefers hidden in the light fixture." Not all jazzmen are like this. Some breed to reproduce the race and have homes and wives. Many settle down and try to be like everyone else. But in the main, the jazzman is a drifter—not rich; not too happy. And dreaming of the big break: his own band, his name in lights over the Paramount, a solid set of records bringing in the money, and beginner brown babes just dying to get inside his arms. But to the average jazzman most of it doesn't happen, and even when it happens to the leaders, the writers of music, the makers of real jazz, it doesn't last —the agents cut it up too fine, the vogue passes, the times get blue and low, and you reach. . . .

The jazzmen are human and have all the human vices. Also, of course, all the human virtues—but no one is much interested in the virtues common to all people. It's much more to the point to see the vices they have in common with other people. The formal attempts to write a jazz history usually try to avoid the subject of drugs and their influence on the music produced. It is true that it's been overdone by some with sensational talk on the subject. But it's also been avoided by a lot of the jazz critics as having little to do with the music produced. Some place between the two schools you will find the truth, but it takes digging and hunting and fact-finding to get it properly in focus.

"Not all jazz-players smoke marijuana or opium, or sniff snow or jab a vein. But jazz players live odd and often strained lives. The living ain't easy; it's troubled with demands and the pressure of the pop-bands, the hasty life and the sudden leavings. Most of the true jazz players are Negroes, and the Negro horn-man or drummer is often on reefers, muggles, grefa, musta, the hemp—all names for the marijuana cigarette which he smokes down to the roach, the smallest butt in the world." The drug is not supposed to be too harmful, and some medical men say it has less harmful effects than hard-drinking. It is the seed of a hemp-like plant that grows wild in many empty lots all over America. The best of it comes from Mexico. It's a big business and the vipers, its peddlers and users, push the sticks at a steady pace. The coarse seeds are made into cigarettes and the user smokes them in big puffs getting high—a state in which time seems to stand still, where the top of the head is filled with all of heaven, and everything seems easy to do, better, stronger and longer. "It helps the beat, it keeps the frenzy, it holds up the strength, it certainly has put a lot of new chords into jazz when you're kicking the gong around. The let-down is slow. You taper off on milk and when it's over, no hangover

. . . just a yen for the next reefer: not habit-forming—just happy memories."

There was no law against its use for a long time, but as the pushers gave it out to school-kids and the peddling of it tied in with the gangster rackets, the big muscle-mobs, it is now against the Federal law to grow, sell or use.

Just how many jazzmen use it? There are some U. S. Government figures that give a clue. A news-report has this to say:

> Though Negroes are only 10% of the U. S. population, they number 45% of narcotic addicts and 75% among the juvenile addicts. The reason, Psychiatrist Walter Adams told the (Negro) National Medical Association in Chicago, is to be found in race discrimination: the use of narcotics is a cover-up for feelings of inferiority, insecurity or depression.

That could mean that the same figures or averages would hold good for the average Negro jazz-band. Maybe a bit higher: the boys are a little more tension-strung than other Negro groups. The figures include, of course, junkies on the hop and all the opium-layout boys, with their yen-box. "Opium pad-parties take time and a place to lay the tea or smoke pad, the cot on which the smoking is done. The little gow hop-pills are rolled between the fingers and cooked on the end of a pin over a *ken-ten* lamp, usually made out of a sardine tin, and a wick and some oil. The pill is cooked until it sizzles and then it is pushed into the bowl of the *yeng-tsiang* pipe and three or four deep big puffs are inhaled before the pill is used up. Three pipes are just about right and then it's drifting and dreamland and everything troubled is far off and of no value. Just this moment counts and this cozy place. Harlem cellars and coal-bins and other places hold a lot of pad-joints where three or four pals can get together to fix each other hop, and dream away the time. Women, money, the real world doesn't matter too much. It's a hard habit to break, expensive to run, and dangerous, as the sweet smell of the cooking pill is a giveaway.

"The junkers sniff it or take it in the arm in the most primitive way. They heat some water in a teaspoon with a match or candle, dissolve into it the white powder of morphine, jab a vein—usually in the arm—with a pin and then with an eyedropper suck up the mixture from the spoon and inject the jolt into the raw arm. The kick hits them at once and they brighten up, their eyes gleam, and they are dangerous. The procedure is also unsanitary, and a cheap junkie's arms and legs are covered with unhealed jabs, often badly infected." The percentage of drug-takers among the jazzplayers is bigger than they will admit, but not as high as some people claim.

The drug talk mixed with jazz-patter is an interesting language. Someone reported the real talk in an interview with a girl viper; she was explaining what it's all about and how it affected her interest in music.

"I'm really turned on, man," she cried. "I'm higher than a giraffe's toupee. I started blasting when I was 13." Her two dogs, she confided, like marijuana too. "When the pups were two months old, I'd blow weed smoke in a paper bag and put it over their heads. I did the same for the canary. Sing? Man, he just dropped over—stoned." Now why, she demanded, was she put in jail merely for "smoking a pot"?

. . . Marijuana, she felt, was neither habit forming nor harmful. But people insisted on acting as though it were bad like getting "lushed" (drunk), and all the squares put you down strong (turned on you). "Those dope stories—all about how you go around killing old ladies when you smoke a pot. It's a real drag. Actually, you just sit around and listen to music. I love Bach. Mozart? No comment. Mendelssohn? How square can you get? *I want it modern.* I want to go to Sweden where it really wails."

Why did she smoke marijuana? "Because it's kicks. It's just like being a lush only you don't have a hangover and you're not sloppy and getting sick and maybe going out and driving a car and killing someone, like a lush. And it's cheaper than Scotch. Two or three people can get high on one joint (marijuana cigarette). Of course, you can take bennies (Benzedrine) or dexies (Dexedrine), but they make me too nervous. I'm a hog. I don't just take one. I take three or four. You can get hooked on them."

Being a "head" is being part of a whole new culture. "Everybody's a head now. One out of every five persons you meet on the street are heads. But all those things they say about them aren't true. There are lots of blowing cats (musicians) who have been smoking for years. Lots of doctors. People aren't the sharpest. They don't catch on. Not even on junk. You know you don't have to stand in the middle of the living-room and say, 'Pardon me, mother, while I have a fix!' Why don't people leave us alone?

"I called my dad and he hung up. My folks have put me down strong so I've put them down strong. Mother is bugged (angry) at me."

Most of the popular jazz-talk among the teen-age cats is no longer used in jazz circles. It's been a long time since a real jazzman greeted a friend with "Slip me some of that skin, gate" or admitted his clarinet was "some licorice-stick." As soon as the outside world takes over some talk, the boys drop it overboard and get some new words working for them. Slang, jargon, argot is the private talk of private groups: safe-crackers, bull-fighters, con-men, hobos, B-girls and experts like engineers who have a lot of technical stuff on their hands. Some of these private languages are from the underworld where the words come up and into popular use with, often, their obscene original meaning toned down. Here are some practical jazz-words:

Jazz is of all kinds, and *mop mop* jazz is the mechanical stuff full of riffs. The white visitor is called an *ofay* by Negroes—their pig-Latin for pig—so that they can keep making cracks about him out loud. He is also known as *ofaginzy,* just to make it harder. The *squares,* the unenlightened, don't get it. A *spade* or a *spaginzy* is a Negro; an *Uncle Tom* is one who caters to white taste, and a *handkerchief-head* is an old-fashioned Negro who doesn't know his rights. Any white man from the South is a *Peckerwood.* And some words that sound almost alike have different meanings. To *scat* is to make nonsense sounds to a song a la Louis Armstrong, but to *scoff* is to eat, and *scuffle* is to get by.

When a jazz-player is *woodshedding,* he is alone, practicing, and when he asks you to "tell a green man," he wants you to put him wise. *Razzmatazz* music is corny jazz, *rinky-dink* is broken-down stuff and the true meaning of *be-bop,* also called *re-bop,* and *rip-bop* is a fast, frenzied and mechanical jazz.

To have a ball is to get by with a good time, and *to beat your chops* is to talk, not to be confused with *blowing your cap,* which is to go mad. *Boogily-boogily* is not to be too confused with *boogie-woogie,* but means pell-mell. *Dicty* is high-class, but *hincty* is an insult, meaning snobbish; *stash* is to hide, a *yardbird* is a low mug and *carrying weight* is a load of the blues.

Women have a lot of special terms in jazz-talk, some of them respectable. But, as in Chaucer, she is often referred to by an image term purely sexual. The sexual act is fully covered, but not in these pages. A song like *Sea Food Mama* that was popular some years ago has another set of meanings in Harlem and along the jazz-belt.

"The *uppity,* the ritzy folk, don't know the half of it about jazz talk. The Savoy Ballroom in Harlem is The Track. Seventh Avenue is The Stroll. *Faust* is not a poem, it means ugly; King Kong is not a movie, it's cheap alcohol, also known as Tigersweat. A *shakeup* is a mixture of corn whisky and wine."

Musically, *groovy* is really good; a *gig* is a one-time playing date. To break time out of tempo is to *brown off.* A *press roll* is played on snare drums, *jim-jam* is to jump it lively. The *flareup* is to build a chord. Nothing at all is the *dooley-squat,* and to hunt fun is to *do it for kicks.* A *freebee* is a mooch or handout; a *blip* is five cents. A *chinch* is a bedbug, usually found in a *padhouse* or bedroom. *Blow your lump* is replacing blow your top. A lot of this talk changes meaning from time to time.

"The jazz talk is private, but a lot of people use it around the cafe spots and Tin Pan Alley and along the reefer route. It's used in hotel bedrooms where they drink and jam, and in the all-night eating places where they grow mellow and maudlin, and the dawn comes up cold like an icebox and they shuffle off to hired rooms to hit the pad and maybe warm up a few blues all alone. New York is The Big Apple,

and when they are playing jazz there, or elsewhere, and alter pitch between notes, they call it scooping-pitch, or bending." *Blue notes* are the flattened thirds and seventh in the blue scale. *Bounce* is a buoyant beat, also known as the *businessman's bounce,* a two-beat played fast. *To bug* is to bewilder, and a *clambake* is a jam session; a *dog-tune* is one that isn't very good music; *to fake* it is to improvise, and to *goof-off* is to let your attention drift. A *mickey mouse band* is a real corny outfit that pushes trombone sounds and uses out-of-tune saxes.

A *moldy fig* is what the longhairs of jazz call a simple admirer of Dixieland jazz. *Ticky* is another word for corny. A *jump band* is a big and powerful jazz-band, a *lick* is a break, and a *rideout* is to swing a last chorus. *To rock* is to jump and swing. *For kicks* is to get pleasure, *a bringdown* is a depressing character.

"There are hundreds of jazz words, but mostly they come and go quickly; they either lack kicks or get taken up by the squares, so new words are coined. At its best, jazz talk is a solid thing expressive as a punch in the nose, close to the life of its users and powerfully impressive in getting you hep to the true meaning. It is not the talk used by criminals, yet criminals borrow from it, and jazz often takes on a con man's word, but changes it slightly for its needs. Like head, for girl."

A suit of clothing is *a set of drapes,* or *a set of threads,* and the best ones are real *zooty,* fashionable. *Freak* is homosexual, and when *everything is George,* everything is all right, and *George* is like saying Right. A *clinker* is a bum-note, *a psychokick* is an erotic excitement, also called *a nympho kick. To latch on* is to grab, to call a man *nappy* is to say his hair is kinky—a real insult.

"The jazz lovers who don't play it have a lot of words that the jazzmen don't use much, but which most people think are real jazz words. Some may have been once but got corny, but most are invention of non-players. *Lip-splitter* for horn-player, *box of teeth* for an accordian, *gas-pipe* for a trombone, *wop-stick* for clarinet, *belly fiddle* for guitar. But *woodpile* for xylophone is real talk, as is *string-whanger* for a guitarist."

Long underwear or *long-hair* or *salon mush* for concert stuff is still in order. A *clambake* is still admitted for a jam session, but *canary* or *mouse* for woman is just used in smart fiction about jazz. *Smear* or *slurp* will do for a glissando. *Hepcat, rug-cutter* are old-fashioned now. An *icky* and *tin-ear* is a man who doesn't like swing. A dance is *cement-mixer,* a good thing is a *killer-diller.* A girl is, lately, *a pig* or *beast;* money is *moula, china* or *folding lettuce.* Anybody fat is *five-by-five,* a sad type is a *cleek,* a *character,* or a *specimen.* Red Hot Mama is from the twenties and not used anymore, *nach* for naturally is also going, as is *terrif, big deal, I got news for you. Meathead, chowderhead* and *waterhead* remain, as do *slotmouth* and *gatemouth,* all terms of disrespect.

Jazz itself, in its original premusical form, had only one meaning: sexual intercourse. A lot of words that were once obscene are now part of jazz talk: *shortnin' bread, seafood, jelly-roll* and *easy rider. Juke* from juke box came from juke house—which was once a whorehouse, now called *cathouse* or *canhouse. Boogie woogie* used to mean the secondary stages of syphilis, and *jitterbug* a sexual reaction to music.

Around the end of 1952, some of those who hung around jazz players, but weren't usually musicians themselves, began to pass around something called the "bop joke." It wasn't bop talk at all but jazz talk, and they tried to explain it like this:

"The essence of bop humor lies in the fact that its creators, carried away by their music, are often in a doped state of ecstasy known as *gone.* Their sense of time is so cockeyed that racing or falling objects seem to be floating by. Violent events become sweet and lovely. The bopster views his world with wonder and joy, and nothing is ever quite what it is. Bop jokes certainly are not everybody's, but those who acquire taste for them feel *cool, gone, crazy* and *stoned.*

"What they mean by gone is usually high, on reefers or booze, or both. The rest of their talk isn't much more than jazz talk extended a bit: *crazy:* new, wonderful, wildly exciting; *cool:* tasty, pretty; *goof:* to blow a wrong note, or to make a mistake; *hipster:* modern version of hepcat; *dig:* to understand, appreciate the subtleties; *stoned:* drunk, drugged, captivated, ecstatic, sent out of this world; *flip:* to react enthusiastically."

Here are some bop jokes that went the rounds, which, if lacking in real humor, at least show the way the language is used. Bopsters in India listen to a snake charmer. "Just dig that cool arrangement!" one exclaims. "Never mind the arrangement," says his pal seeing the wriggling cobra. "Dig that crazy music stand!"

Two bopsters go into a joint. One orders a piece of pie. Says the waitress, "The pie is gone." "Oh, that crazy pie!" cries the bopster. "I'll take *two* pieces!"

Two bopsters are stoned in a hotel penthouse. One says, "Man,

I feel so great I could walk right out on that cloud!" He steps out the window. When the police arrive, one asks the second bopster why he let his friend jump. "Man," he replies, "I thought he could make it!"

Professors have traced, they say, some vocabulary of the West African Gullahs into jazz talk, but actually most of the terms were local and invented on the spur of the moment. Jazz, like Chaucer or Shakespeare or the poetry of Villon, the texts of James Joyce or the later D. H. Lawrence, used what was handy in folk-talk and what was expressive, to get more vitality into the language. Words wear out, become too polite, and so fresh blood must come from the places where man is actively fighting for survival, burdened by vice and frustrations. Respectable, well-off people don't invent new words. They are doing fine with what they have, they want no change, so the creative artist has often been forced to the underworld for his more expressive phrases, because only there will he be accepted without question as a member of society. Most new expressions of the arts and the criminal underworld are mutually acceptable to each other. Even if often only on the sexual level, they seem to sense that for the full moral sin, you must first practice the psychological sin.

They understand the poetry and fact of:

Baby, see that spider climbin' on the wall,
He's goin' up there for to get his ashes hauled.

Or the direct symbolism of:

You're playin' in my orchard now don't you see
If you don't like my peaches, stop shakin' my tree.
Oh, tell me how long, how long must I wait?
Oh, can't I get it now? or must I hesitate . . .?

But what is beyond mere words or morals? Jazz, when pure and blue, means something special to the jazzman. As he plays it he splits our world into the full river of the spectrum—into a flood rich, strange, beautiful—not to be labelled as any Tin Pan Alley mail-order mysticism. He knows that the real artist tries to conduct his life so as to fully realize one's self. He doesn't always succeed.

At its best, the maker of jazz knows the world can never purge itself of its monsters. Jazz, when healthy, never retreats into the nihilism of just noise, or the sterile world of the soundbenders. The real jazzman is introspective, tough and oblique—perhaps he will continue to be so, to remember that both seed-time and harvest in music are not a matter of the usual one season of sowing and reaping.

His music, his lost music, or found music, solves many of the problems of modern life—he shows how to live, often, with a theme of guilt, lost innocence, economics, the themes of redemption and the twilight of old values—of cheapness, or mediocrity.

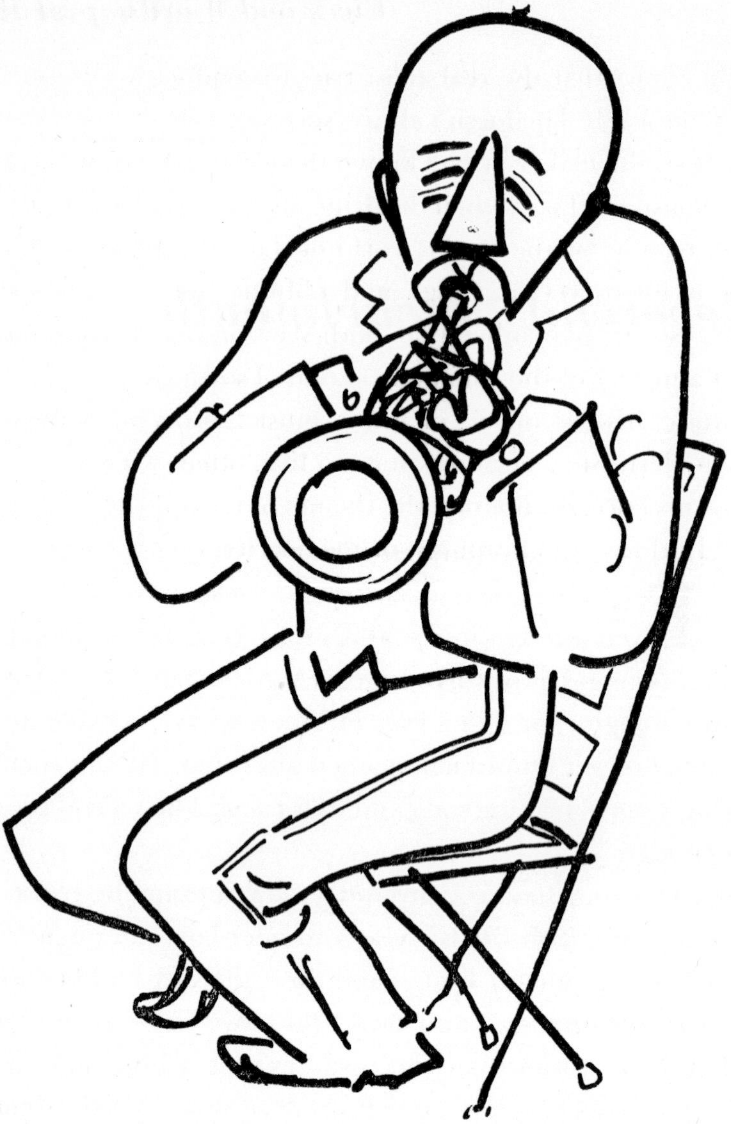

Close the doors!
They're comin' through the windows.
Close the windows!
They're comin' through the doors . . .
THE HEEBEES

Chapter 19

The Reverend Satchelmouth

Even a mug often realizes that what start as biological actions can often end as historical ideas. A great man doesn't have to invent a steam-engine, or win a war. He doesn't have to make love to Helen of Troy or get a mustache named after him. He can spend his life blowing a horn, making song and music and if he's a real great man—that's enough."

Louie Armstrong has been around a long time and he's lasted. "He wasn't last year's flash or this year's wonder-boy. Through the years he's managed to remain Louie, and do it the way he likes and now he's grown full-sized and you could no more write about jazz without a close look at him than you could explain a blue note to a deaf man. There has been less nonsense talked and written about Louie than almost any other jazzman. What he sells is plain to hear, and he goes about it without any fancy frills. His music is true because the man is cut true, and big and black and solid."

He came in just after the century started, and New Orleans saw a lot of him growing up, learning music, making noise. "It was New Orleans of the old days, which means it wasn't as shabby as it is now in the old parts, or as fashionable as it is now in the new parts. It was, for him, a hungry tough town, but he got started, and he went.

"While New Orleans was letting in the Near Year, 1913, Louie Armstrong, twelve years old, had been running around town singing tenor (forgive him) with a Perdido Street quartette. Storyville knew Louie as a kid—and his side-kicks, Happy, Shots and Kid Rena. They got pushed around, and their tails run out of the district, but they came back—Louie ashamed of his tenor, dreaming of singing bass, playing a four-string guitar, home-made of a flat-wood neck, copper wires stripped from some unsuspecting source, a cigarbox body. He lived near the place where Buddy Bolden's band warmed up, and he learned to whistle in time with the players."

Louie spent his time away from the Waif's Home on a Vieux Carré cart of stove coal, shouting:

My mule is white
My face is black!
I sells my coal
Two bits a sack!

"The Home wasn't too bad, and lots of kids got picked up just to get use of the free band instruments. Louie got a cornet from Joseph Jones, Captain of the Waif's Home. Louie had already learned to blow the damn thing. But at the Home he had time to get the playing down the way he liked it. He cut notches in the cornet mouthbit so it would keep firm against his lip. He blew it until his own lip became tough enough to do away with the need of notches." Peter Davis at the home taught Louie to read, says one account, but it doesn't make it clear if that meant school reading, or music.

He came out of the Home a good horn-player, but too young to get a band job. He shot crap, peddled papers, ran sordid errands and there was, of course, the coal racket—filling a gunny with coal dropped by loaders on river barges. There was always a way to make two bits, but never much more.

"Louie was growing stocky and hard, and he had a girl, Daisy Parker. She liked to swing her fists and mix it up, and Louie learned to duck. He and Daisy did the dance spots and sat by the Eagle Bandstand and listened to Bunk Johnson play that cornet. Louie got a few spots playing horn in dives around Gravier Street, maybe knocking down a buck a night." Joe Oliver was coming right along and in 1917 Louie was studying his style and trying to copy it. Louie organized a band in the Oliver style with little Joe Lindsay. It wasn't easy to break in with great hornmen like Bunk and Oliver around.

"Louie somehow found himself married to Daisy and still ducking. When things got too lippy at home, he went on the river with Fate Marables' *Jazz-E-Saz Band."* It was good on the big Strekfus line boats, with the big boating parties and good men working with him—Pop Foster, Dave Jones, Baby Dodds, Picou, Sam Dutrey. After a season or so on the Mississippi, Louie settled in on Burgundy Street with Zut Singleton's band at the Orchard Cabaret. Then he went over to Tommy Anderson's *Real Thing,* on Rampart Street. Louie was trying his hand at writing music now and he got a whole fifty dollars for his rights to *I Wish I Could Shimmy Like My Sister Kate.* Louie was growing up, growing into a great horn man, getting ahead in his music.

"One summer day in 1922, there came a telegram from Joe Oliver, in Chicago, for Louie to get himself up there and play second cornet in King Oliver's band. It was the bigtime for Louie, who packed his bag and came and fitted right in with the music—giving Joe plenty of trouble with a good horn. But Joe enjoyed it even if he knew this twenty-two-year-old-boy was going to outplay him some day.

"Lil Hardin kind of took the gatemouthed Louie under her wing. Lil had brain and education and hadn't planned to play anything but classical piano, but here she was, making jazz history. She began by playing piano in a music store for three whole dollars a week. She played first for *Sugar John's New Orleans Jazz Band,* then King Oliver latched onto her. And she fell for Louie, and Louie liked her. Daisy seems to have become the ex-Mrs. Armstrong about this time. Nobody knows just how it all worked emotionally. But it seemed proper and fitting and legal.

"In February, 1924, Lil and Louie were married. Lil worked the fat off Louie. She got a book of the standard cornet solos and drilled him. He really worked, and he even took lessons from a krauthead down at Kimball Hall, who showed Louie all the European cornet clutches. But Louie just took what he wanted. He got to be a damn good sight-reader. When he began to record, he could use the music or wipe it off. Louie played a lot of everything he had learned, but he was becoming an artist in his own right, whistling the riffs that were to become a kind of trademark of the Armstrong style. He shifted from cornet to trumpet and back."

In 1924 Louie got to New York, where he worked at Roseland with Fletcher Henderson. "It was too rich for Louie—too big—he rattled around in that band. He blew a good horn, but he couldn't just fill in or stretch out and his work was better than the band's as a whole. Louie just bided his time. Henderson was a little too sweet and soft for him." But when he went recording with Maggie Jones and Clarence William's *Blue Five* and the *Red Onion Jazz Babies, Coal Cart Blues, Texas Moaners, Cake-Walking Baby* are real Basin Street.

"Lil put together her own band in Chicago, *Lil's Dreamland Syncopators,* starring, modestly, 'Louis Armstrong, World's Greatest Jazz Cornetist.' He blew it good and right, gut-bucket, gully-low horn-playing." Then Louie went over to the Vendome and became the singing actor, the shouting, moaning voice projecting over the hot horn and the ever-ready handkerchief. Using the big scarred lip, the slit-eyed smile that was to make him as famous a reciter-singer as a horn-player. It's an amazing thing the way he handles himself—the gutteral laugh, the husky moaning, the scattering of the words into pure Gertrude Stein, the incoherent patter that replaces the words—a performance that is never ham. It may not be art, it isn't, certainly, real true jazz, but it's a good show. And behind it all was the horn-playing, and that never let down. But with horn or as the Reverend Satchelmouth, he was always Louie.

Louie didn't let New Orleans down. He set up the *Hot Five* for Okeh sides, and did a lot of things—some of it a little sleek and smooth, often sweet, but between the stuff they cut for the trade, you would find a few great records. *Savoy Blues, Wildman Blues, Potato Head Blues, Gut-Bucket Blues, Drop That Sack, Put 'em Down Blues.* It was still tailgate trumpet and Rampart Street cornet.

The *Hot Five* became the *Hot Seven,* knocking out *Gully Low Blues, Alligator Crawl, King of the Blues.* "It was a good time, with everyone very informal, the bottle of gin, and everybody willing to try anything and maybe record it if it seemed worth it. The recording takes were ruined a lot (but maybe they threw away the best to get it in the popular groove). It was good electric recording, and now it's all part of jazz history. Louie's name was up in lights at the Sunset Cafe, and he was the star, but everybody got their chance and a lot of things happened those Chicago winter nights before spring came and they opened the sealed cafe windows and let the sound escape for the season.

"Louie was being seriously published by Melrose, as an example of what every young horn-player should know: *Fifty Hot Choruses of Armstrong.* It broke a lot of teeth and bashed in the lips of many a young punk trying on the master's methods.

"Louie moved around a lot, made money, made friends and played the best he knew how, and his best was very good. He was famous now; he got a hundred a night for special events, and his regular salary was two hundred dollars a week. Louie had a big yellow roadster and he and Zutty and Hines managed to reach New York in it. They replaced Ellington for a time, then opened at the Savoy in Harlem. They went to Connie's Inn. Louie even did time in the Broadway revue, *Hot Chocolates.*

"After that, Louie toured, and there was only one thing to do. Go to Europe, and so Louie did. Europe liked what it heard and the big new interest in jazz in Europe that grew up in the early thirties can be blamed on Louie's tour. He enjoyed it, they enjoyed it and the French jazz fiends became experts all over Europe, and began to write books about jazz, mostly without knowing anything about the early New Orleans music.

"Louie had come a long way from selling coal, playing in reform school, copying Bunk and Oliver. He's been lucky and he knows it. He didn't get tossed aside like Bunk to tote cotton and work the fields. He didn't die because he couldn't pay doctor bills like Oliver, rattling around in a broken-down bus, forgotten, his best stuff swiped. No, Louie is around, bigger, darker and happier than ever. He's a maker of fine music and while we haven't and aren't going to decide if jazz is or is not a great art, he is certainly one of the best it has. He's got a feel and an endurance, he's got the big lungs, the supply of air, he's got the big lip. He can pump or relax that throat, but all that is only the stuff he uses. What else he gets out of his body and his horn can't be explained so easy. The values of his glissandi, the virtuosity in the high register. Even his tricks aren't just tricks. He never stops trying, and never stops practicing. He's beautiful to hear—he's warm and alive. He's a bridge between the Bolden music and the modern schools, a kind of traveler in time between the old things and what they're trying to do. He hasn't gone as far off as Bix and Ellington in trying to make it concert, but he isn't ready to sit in the rut of the past. Louie is willing to try new effects, new music. He started with cornet and became a trumpet man. And no matter how big it was, he was able to handle it. He is the master of that delay in rhythmic accents and intervals, so that when he is swinging it away from the regular beat, he's often at his best. Louie can do things in melodic variation; his solos, filled with fast runs and descending sections and blue breaks, look easy. And it is easy for him because of his simplicity no matter how involved the music. When Louie is using just one pitch, getting his effects with crescendos, we are hearing jazz horn at its best so far. He makes his blues more than vocal, he makes them personal. Like all true artists, his timing is perfect and the casual effects he seems to brush against never leave him making a mistake. There is also a silent music in his playing, those rests and breaks that are as shrill and nerve-tormenting as the one he hits."

Louie is more than an influence; he has the virtue most great jazzmen lack—survival. He has managed to stay around. The jinx that beat down Buddy Bolden, that hasseled King Oliver, so far hasn't touched this man, or his vibrato. He seems to be producing music with his consciousness, but it is often produced by his past—all the long road up, the far way he has come, the music he had brought along, the scat-talk, the whistling, the word-patters that dance on his tongue. "And there it all is—the shining trumpet that he holds like destiny in his meathooks, the white badge of handkerchief that he fumbles, the big broad face, and the teeth he parts slightly in the middle." If he weren't so human, he'd be a symbol of the jazzman, not coming of age (for jazz is too young for that) but of one of those who bent back the horizon and let a little fresh air and sound into the fields of the republic.

I'd rather drink muddy water, Lord,
Sleep in a hollow log
Than be up here in New York
Treated like a dirty dog . . .

MAKIN' FRIENDS BLUES

Chapter 20

Home to Harlem

Some jazzmen don't conform—they seem to know that conformists wear themselves out in repressing energies that should be used in art. "In Harlem they don't conform much. There are two Harlems, one is the phony one for the thrill seekers, out to be nice to the Negroes and tell them what a great folk-art they have; the hunters for thrills, 'trade,' and a little excitement to talk about below the dark belt. The other Harlem is real: sad, gay, a slum and a world they never made but got trapped in. It looms big and wide, and it has its fancy places and its low places, and the rent is always too high. It has Negroes who are converted Jews, and also Fascist storm-troopers trying to pass as Arabs. It has its own newspapers and culture and they even collect Picassos and read T. S. Eliot, and they also have killers and vipers selling a smoke-pot to school kids. It's good, it's bad and it's musical.

"Harlem isn't a unit or a city within a city. It's a country, a colored country surrounded by New York City, and like any country you can't label it from any one of its parts. There was a colored actor, Canada Lee, who played on stage in white face. And Father Divine figured out a way for God to make a buck now and then.

"To a million people it is home: 'where you go and they have to let you in.' They walk the streets and sit on the steps. And the kids play kick-the-stick and robbing Brinks, in the gutters."

The heart of Harlem is big, noisy and dirty and centers around One Hundred Thirty-first Street and Seventh Avenue. "The Corner is where the housewives pass with their shopping bags, where the hincty numbers boys and the poolroom characters stand in a fancy set of threads," where the lovers of women and horses exist in the spotty sun, resting between pleasures. You can walk along The Stroll—that block between One Hundred Thirty-first and One Hundred Thirty-second Street, and taste and hear how far the Negro has come since the New Orleans days.

"Some of that old love of juju and voodoo is around: fortune-tellers, star-gazers and the Tree of Hope—at least what's left of the Tree after they all touched it and said their wishes to it and tapped it. And sometimes it worked, as good as a holy relic of a rotting saint's arm, or buying a novena downtown at St. Pat's."

"Seventh Avenue, Harlem, the Main Stroll with the big watermelon-colored Cadillacs and Lincolns of the prizefighters, the kink-remover makers and numbers' racket sharks. And the busted-down jalopies of the small jazz-bands coming in or going out to pick-up dates among the Jersey speaks and roadhouses. It all smelled busy, and the decaying buildings owned by respectable church-going white folk stank and smoked and rotted. The small fry sat on the curbs sucking colored ices, one roller-skate on the right foot. The eating places were busy with the old-remembered food. Hominy and grits, chitlin's, Brunswick stew and ribs barbequed in a smoldering sauce. The vipers standing under the Tree of Hope peddling golden gage, remembering when it wasn't a crime to push muta."

"Barbershops, the Performers and Entertainers Club, with the dicty set shaved smooth down to a one-hairline mustache. Connie's Inn, the old Lafayette with a beautiful yellow babe shaking it as she walked slowly down the alley, the cellar of the Hoofers' Club with a battered radio calling the winner of the third at Belmont. Tabb's Restaurant with some handkerchief heads and kids without shoes getting paper bags of hand-outs through the back door. The Rhythm Club with the droop of a mop-mop trombone being played in a casual riffy way, all alone, before the boys get together as a group. The Barbeque with the good smells, and the upstairs halls where they shuffled for jobs, stole music, and a lot of good rehearsing went on. You could put the bite on Erskine Hawkins, Jimmy Lunceford or Cab Calloway on the stairs, no touch less than four bits. The Lafayette's backstage door on the alley near the bar of the Bandbox, where you could buy the well-stacked stage babes a drink, and where there were always a few of the boys with a horn in a paper-bag, or a naked-looking string bass being carried around by a small player with no place to lay the two of them down that night. *Bury you now—dig you later. . . .*"

"That was Harlem as it was, and later the smart white folk, the ofaginzys, came, in tails and white ties, hunting kife, jazz, tall tea, a chance of luck or the newest verse to *Minnie The Moocher.* They were snobs, said words like Freud, Noel Coward, Harding, but they had money and everyone who didn't racket, peddle or hustle was usually mighty hungry in those years when Wall Street laid down dead.

"Coldwater flats, yard toilets, no glass in the windows and six to a bed; relief checks and charity food, tattered men on street corners with no work to be had. A woman with big sad eyes, the kid with rickets and a spot on the lung, trying to sweet-talk someone out of a bottle of milk. And all this time they were making music, blue music, hot music, what is now Harlem jazz, New York style—but still, in its way, an American music, smoky around the edges. . . . You can correct the poet—*this* is the way a world ends: not with a bang, but a blue note."

To real jazz, the symbolism of its dreams is not allegory disguising truth but rather new truths freshly invented. New York City was the longest way jazz had yet come from early New Orleans. And it was in New York that swing was to change the flow of the original blend, make it something it wasn't and make it something that might or could become a new way of playing it. To a lot of people swing is the throwing away of the honest Negro elements of jazz, shoving in its place a lot of the easy popular stuff that a white society can accept as music just a little politer than the true and original forms.

A lot of this is true. New York did change jazz and not always for the best. But jazz had to meet Tin Pan Alley and pop bands and all the crumby stuff that is radio, TV and vaudeville. It couldn't live any more in its blue tower, lonely but pure on the delta. To be a real force, it had to take on the big town and fight it out—slug it out. And that's what happened in New York. Jazz took a few steps back—which doesn't mean it was licked for there were, even there, plenty of playing cats who kept it pure and kept it making progress.

Dixieland in New York put up a good fight. There were early type Dixieland bands like the *Original Hot Five* in 1923, and men like Jim Moynahan and his clarinet, and Brad Gowans and his trombone. Combos like the *Goofus Five, Little Ramblers, California Ramblers* and *Birmingham Aces, Cotton Pickers,* and *Ladd's Black Aces.* Good men there, too: Phil Napoleon, trumpet; Miff Mole, Vince Grande, trombones; Jimmy Lytell, clarinet; Frank Signorelli, piano; and Jack Roth, drums.

"They worked with half-arranged music, a somewhat crude phrasing. They weren't as wild as Chicago style. It's too easy to say Dixieland is the intellectual way of music, and Chicago the emotional; all good music is a lot of each. By 1926, the *Memphis Five* kind of music was being beaten out by swing. The *Memphis Five,* like the Chicago style, has been kicked around by the critics who think only Negroes can play real jazz. But they were more than junk-pile players, they had a solid Dixieland bass. It was a good band and an honest one. It was a hybrid, half jackass, half horse. In its own way it was true to

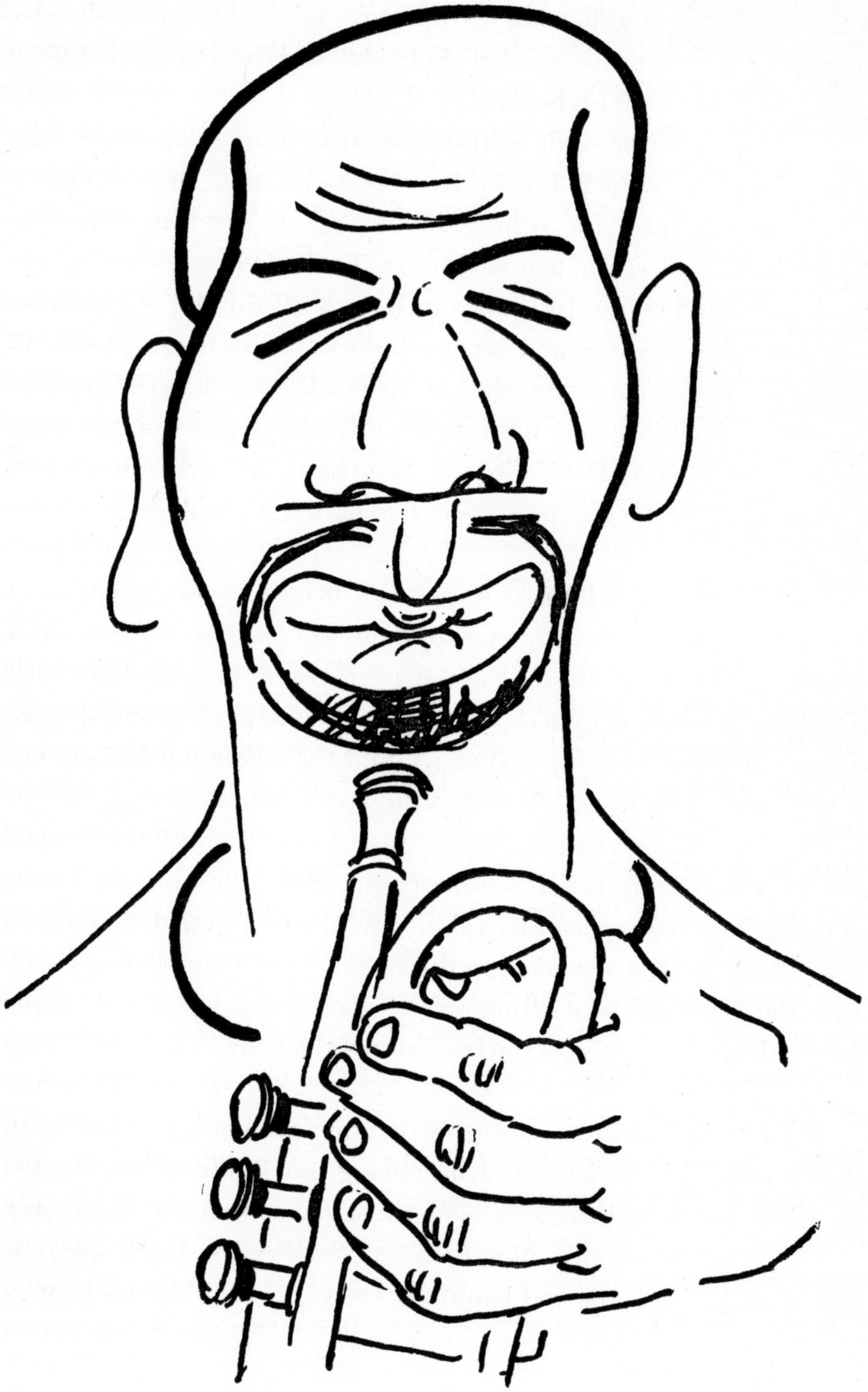

good jazz but it couldn't last as the white folk—the ofay mob—discovered Harlem and demanded their idea of jazz, and got it full of psycho kick and freakish byplay.

"By 1926, the vo-de-o-do style of Bix's *Wolverines* was taking over a lot of New York. Loring Red Nichols, one of Bix's followers, was setting the pace for awhile. The arranging was heavy, the solo featured the style very much vo-de-o-do. The style is very close now to big hincty band swing. Just how much harm all this did is a question you can talk a week on and get no closer to the facts except that all music has its popular times when it isn't really popular crud, and yet isn't its original form any more. Sweet swing certainly came in when Jimmy and Tommy Dorsey joined the groups, and from then on it's hard to separate the groups as every one played in combos with everyone else.

"By 1933, Dixieland-Chicago had become pretty much sweet swing. The band stays firmly on the beat, the syncopation is made as simple as you can get it. The crooner has gotten into the horns, the trombone is minding its manners and has become sleek, the reed of the clarinet is getting cloying and sweet, and the whole musical pattern is swift and decorative. It's still music and a new way of playing it. You may not like it compared to the early music for it's house-broken and matches the drapes. It's droopy. The flash, the bite, the elastic phrasing has been replaced by a skilled sentimental accent. Some good men taking jazz down worked in this mood. Artie Shaw, Benny Goodman, the Dorseys, Duke Ellington. It's good music but lots of people don't think it's jazz. It's got the face but not the body."

The jazz Negroes, always struggling economically and fighting a hostile white society, came into swing, too. But in the main it was the white boys who generaled swing into replacing the old solid jazz.

"The *Mound City Blue Blowers* came from St. Louis with scat singing and trick kazoo and banjo work. Led by Red McKenzie, they spread their gospel even to London. They retained some of the rhythmic stuff of jazz, but crossed it with a kind of hillbilly vaudeville. Sweet harmony replaced the old ideas and became monotony.

"Coleman Hawkins kept two styles going—a slow and fast-climbing scale arpeggios that led no place, and a blowing, rising and falling multo-note fury. Glenn Miller took the Teagarden and Jimmy Harrison trombone styles and made big loud solos that connected only slightly with jazz. The solos in many bands were becoming salon acts, improvisations that lacked the logic of the real New Orleans or Dixieland truths.

"What became New York Dixieland in white hands and Harlem style with the Negroes lost its roots. White jazz accepted the violin. Paul Whiteman and Jean Goldkette, who played a good pseudo-jazz, loaded up on string sections. Joe Venuti, a good fiddler, came in and jazz took on a lot of Tin Pan Alley. The vo-de-o-do, the rhythmic stress, but little syncopation of polyrhythm were the thing for the uppity listener.

"While New York was going to swing, jazz was moving around and setting up groups among the followers of New Orleans and Dixieland style. At first they were misled by the popular bands and based their ideas of jazz on the popular versions and didn't even know about Buddy Bolden and King Oliver and all the rest.

"There had been jazz in Europe during World War I when the Negro troops brought over their musical feeling and forms. *Jim Europe's Band* during that war got them used to the brass and of course Louie Armstrong had been over and they liked it a lot and took to Louie and his horn. A kind of French jazz had been around for some time, and Sidney Bechet had done a good pioneer effort.

"The result could only be (around 1930) of the organizing of the Hot Club of France, and its string quintette, made up of string bass, three guitars and violin. It was certainly different and at first was mighty odd jazz. If it was jazz. But in its way it was another offshoot of white music based on jazz and it did no harm. The gypsy guitarist Django Reinhardt was an amazing performer and improvisatory as hell. They never learned to play Negro style and they were trapped when they took on brass and wood by their local training as to tone and method."

The jazz influence in Europe upset the apple-cart of a lot of long-haired Mittel Europa composers and they called their work jazz opera, or jazz poems, concertos and rhapsodies. Krenek did an opera in blackface, *Jonny Spielt Auf,* that didn't get any place as new music and wasn't much opera and just acted like jazz. There was Milhaud's *Creation du Monde* and Berg's *Wozzeck.* They tried.

Back home there was the very talented George Gershwin, lost between what the poet would call a world dying and a world coming to birth. He produced *A Rhapsody in Blue* and *Concerto in F.* Gershwin was no doubt a genius, at least the nearest modern music in America has yet had. But his high class concert jazz, and his popular music did nothing for pure jazz—except to make the debased form more popular in Tin Pan Alley. His jazz opera, *Porgy and Bess,* was closer to the Hebrew chants of his own race than to real Negro music. It is clever and steals a few real Negro street cries, but the form is really the old-fashioned white minstrel show using actual Negroes and telling a borrowed story; a white man's idea of Negro life. *Cabin in the Sky* makes the same earnest mistakes. Gershwin's music is good music, but it has no real foundation in Negro folk art.

The European violin tried to hold on to jazz in the work of Eddie South and Stuff Smith. It was moody and carried over into the smooth salon swing of the post-Gershwin school of the Benny Goodman Trio, Quartet and Quintette. Red Norvo and Adrian Rollini were also of this school. The men are all fine makers of music, but the full power is missing in their work. It is often thin and empty, and is usually only good in the solos when they try to reach the New Orleans manner. The fancy work, the effete stuff, crept in—like when Teagarden in *Junk Man* used a swing harp. And in *I Used to Be Above Love,* Artie Shaw made up a string quartet trying to kid chamber music.

Benny Goodman, Tommy Dorsey and Glenn Miller developed an odd kind of guilt-complex. They play two ways: hot riffs *and* sweet swing. They were expert music-makers who managed to eat their cake and still keep a bit—a small bit.

The Negroes got into the sweet swing around 1929 for keeps with Lionel Hampton and the *Chocolate Dandies* and John Kirby and Teddy Wilson. Benny Carter and others began to change the use of the horns; they often all sounded like saxophones. The sweet hot stuff was a network of solos, a jumpy suppressed epileptic style. It's going too far, however, to say the players became introverted and neurotic. A lot of good creative men are neurotic, and were, even in the prime of New Orleans music.

"Harlem style became swing and James P. Johnson and Fats Waller played it the best they knew how. They used a rocking rhythm. *Red Hot Dan, Harlem Fuss, The Minor Drag* are full of good and bad things. But it's exciting to listen to, for all its faults. When Fats got together with Condon, Krupa, Teagarden, Russell and Allen in such things as *Lookin' Good But Feelin' Bad* and *Yellow Dog Blues,* the Negro style and the Chicago style managed to get along very well. Fats liked to jive, clown, but he never let up on his talent. New York jazz was to have its ups and downs, and was to produce nothing as new and exciting as Dixieland and New Orleans style. Harlem never had the freedom to create its own music. It grew too fancy and the whites moved in on it and demanded popular music."

Make my bed
An' light the light.
I'll arrive late tonight—
Black Bird, Bye-bye . . .
BLACK BIRD BYE-BYE

Chapter 21

They Called It Bop

When Wingy Mannone, the Dixieland trumpeter, first heard Dizzy Gillespie, the bop trumpeter, he lettered this sign and placed it outside his own door:

INSIDE WINGY MANNONE. COME IN
AND HEAR THE REAL TRUTH!

"The truth seems to be not that jazz changes too much, but that it didn't change enough. The basic music has been the same for the last fifty years and what they hung on it, unlike painting and literature and poetry, didn't advance it enough. Of course, the rest of art has been around a few thousand years and we see it in the long alley of the historian. Jazz is too new and we can't get far enough away from it to see the curve of the earth on the horizon. We know the curve is there, but can't catch it yet."

St. Louie woman wid her diamond rings
Pulls that man around by her apron strings . . .
I hates to see that evening sun go down
'Cause my baby he done left this town . . .

Ships in de ocean
Rocks in the sea—
Red-headed woman
Made a fool out of me.

"The trouble isn't that we've changed the old jazz songs, we haven't written new ones as good. But that's trying to rush nature and nature, like an ever-lovin' woman, knows it's better when you take your time. The trouble with talking about new jazz from old is that when you get to about this point in the story you usually begin to clutter up with hundreds of names of bands, players, singers and small new ideas about jazz. Many of them were very good. All were solid performers if you get the right lists, but none of them was really a true genius who raised the form of jazz any higher. They just played it well, kept it alive, sang it out and made it stay. Some got rich and some poor, and mostly they died, a lot of them, in a not very pleasant way. The books on jazz give out hundreds of pages listing players and music, recordings and dates, and in the end this detail drives off the casual reader, confuses most of the students and, as for the fanatic, it is never complete enough for him, nor accurate enough. And anyway all that belongs in catalogues.

"Bop is one of those things. It's either an advance in jazz, or it's bad for jazz. But you have to talk about it or the picture would not be complete.

"Bop didn't happen one rainy afternoon with the windows nailed down and gin open and reefers smoking. . . . It grew from the main body of jazz and a lot of people had a lot to do with it. Billy Eckstine for one. Not just as a singer but as a bandman too. His band was once part of Earl Hines' group when he reorganized it in 1934. Dizzy Gillespie joined the band, too, and Dizzy did as much as anyone to make it bop. Bop came into jazz when Dizzy got around to singing in octave jump phrases. He took a triplet with the first and third notes kept an octave below the second. The last two notes when the band took them could sound like *Bu-dee-laht*. . . or maybe *bu-re-bop*. Somebody called this ending *rebop,* but nobody knows how it came to be called *bebop,* unless maybe it sounded better that way. That's how bebop was born, and that's how it was first played. If you're for it, it's great, the new cool jazz; if you don't like it, it stinks. Rather than explain it in detail, listen to Dizzy sing *Salt Peanuts!*

"Coleman Hawkins, playing at Kelly's Stable, heard it and liked it. He and Dizzy made some records for Bluebird—*Woodyn You, Disorder at the Border, Rainbow Mist*—that settled bop as a pattern.

"Billy Eckstine's band was pure bop. Dizzy led a band of his own playing bop in 1945. It was the *Three Deuces.* He and others recorded such bop sides as *Shaw Enough, Hot House* (which was just a bopped-up version of Cole Porter's *What Is This Thing Called Love*), *Blue N' Boogie, Groovin' High* (once *Whisperin'*) and *Dizzy Atmosphere.*

"So bop was on its way and didn't have many friends; just a lot of jumping fiends. It was called 'neuroses in rhythm' and Dizzy and his followers got into the bop uniform. It called for real home-grown goatees on the chin, horn-rimmed glasses and berets. You could wear spats if you dared and maybe carry a cane. When the words were hard, or you felt you didn't need them, you sang out phrases like *Co-pappa-da, Oolva-koo, Oo-bop-sh-bam.* It killed the listening cats.

"A man named Tadd Dameron, often called The Disciple, expanded bop, feeling it could lead to something better. He wrote the music the bop players used, arranging new and old stuff his way. He's behind Dizzy's and Eckstine's and George Auld's versions of *Good Bait, I Can't Get Started, Air-Mail Special, Don't Take Your Love From Me* and *You're Not The King.*"

"A lot of good men went over to bop; a lot more good men didn't. It went up fast, and bop was the rage, and then it simmered down. Maybe it could have gone places if bop had brought out a genius or two. It certainly had some very good men in it. But it lacked the great artists to make it a new, big step up for jazz. It was exciting, or you hated it."

One expert, Louie Armstrong, reported this in an interview: "I'd never play this here bebop, because why? I don't like it . . . bebop is the easy way out. . . . Instead of holding notes the way they should be held, they just play a lot of little notes. They sort of fake out of it. . . . They never learned right. It's all just flash. It don't come from the heart the way real music does."

"In March, 1946, bop was banned from radio station KMPC in Los Angeles. *Time,* a magazine, said bop was 'hot jazz overheated, with overdone lyrics full of bawdiness, references to narcotics and doubletalk.' (This is also true of jazz itself, a lot of the Bible, the followers of psychoanalysis, and almost any man and woman in love.)

"Bop was not all failure to many people, and it was, at times, earnest and real to some of its players and makers. Jazzmen had worked it out and while they still couldn't lift jazz higher than it had been in its classic days, they could understand it a bit more." The best of them saw it was simple, almost like a parable, but the best of it is not diminishing and becoming vulgar ("sex and hunger and loneliness and drink and dope are not vulgar—they are tragic"). They saw the dimensions and measure of jazz, and from the hard life and the hard way it grew, they saw a lot of it as a concept of what you might call luck. Not the easy luck of finding a dollar or keeping a job but luck that was more than mere chance. A magic power, almost, that some happy people had and some unlucky lacked. And jazz could use that kind of luck. Jazz grew to try and take care of its luck, to respect and hoard it, and keep ideals about it, because if you didn't it blew away like goofer-dust. Greed, accumulated cunning, the strong arm stuff, got you no place in jazz. It had to be real life and put down and blown out and knotted in chords.

"Life in jazz (as any place else) was the embodiment of a cluster of themes gravely and honestly done." You couldn't win in the end, maybe, but you could survive and to survive was to stay, to remain. Life and jazz led in the end to tragedy; the price of living comes high, and you pay again and again until the deep six in the graveyard ends all your troubles. But that end is only a plot of ground, six deep and six long. The jazz player is happy to survive and willing to go on living, but he buys no fairy-tales, not for long.

"So if jazz moves slowly, makes mistakes, deep down perhaps it's the stuff they made Greek plays out of, and big noble mottos, and some large ideas about life."

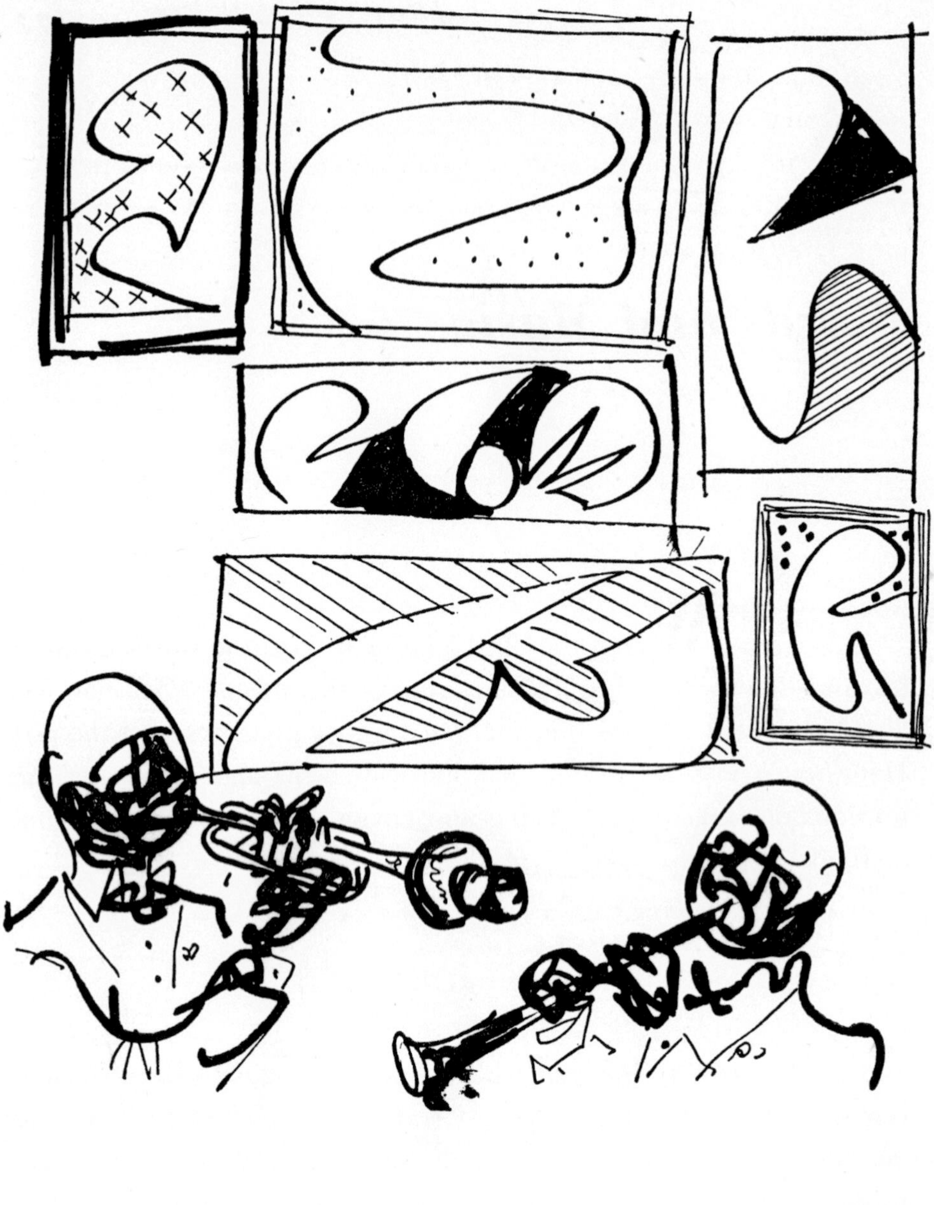

Let her go, let her go, God bless her!
Wherever she may be,
She may roam the whole world over
She'll never find a sweet man like me . . .

ST. JAMES INFIRMARY

Chapter 22

Words and Music

When they first played it, jazz, the words meant a lot, and they added up to the meaning of the music—what man felt about the tragic awe of life, the grace under pressures, and the girl Hemingway says we all once had and called nostalgia. But later the music could take any old thing and change it to its jazz mood and method.

Chinatown, my Chinatown,
Where the lights are low.
Hearts that know no other land
Drifting to and fro . . .

"It was what you did with it, not the original stuff, that mattered. Modern painting and poetry said it first: 'get away from nature and ideas, the absolute is a bum. Give everything to surface and technique and form.' That's a fight that's still going on and maybe it will be proven right, and perhaps wrong. But in jazz it caused trouble and almost every day they wrote it off, and said it was finished. But they were wrong because we can only see with the eyes of our time, our prejudices and our personal body chemistry. What is truth? is no longer asked. Truth was the atom and when you cracked that, you got a lot of bits, and it's going to take time to understand all the bits. But whatever they said, they didn't—or couldn't—kill jazz or send it to the museums. Not yet.

"Jazz is still alive and kicking with the same gestures of New Orleans or Dixieland, trying, as usual, to get the feel and the taste of living into its notes; and not politely either." It's like the literary form called the novel. It was a dog for a long time, it grew great and then everyone said it's best days were behind it and no one was writing great novels any more and who needed it, anyway? But it wasn't the novel that was dead, it was the novelists. "So jazz isn't dead, just most of the great players and inventors. There's been a hassle about what was right and what was wrong with jazz, but the reasons don't matter if you can turn up a Bolden, a Laine, an Oliver, a Bunk Johnson, a Louie Armstrong; turn up a lot of them and turn them loose.

"Jazz just got too fashionable for a time. It moved over to France around 1930, and the same mob that had almost buried modern art with their explaining of Negro carving, moved in to explain how great jazz was and why Americans just didn't know it. The best of the mob was Hugues Panassie, a good scholar and clear thinker." He wrote two books about it, *Le Jazz Hot* (1934) and *The Real Jazz* (1942). "He got himself into a knot with the first one when he overlooked all of the early Negro jazz in New Orleans. He got better in the second book but somehow, Basin Street doesn't translate very well into French. It was a serious try and it did no harm, but it's feeble stuff—long-distance guessing."

"Nobody knows how many recordings were made, how many masters are still around for original pressings. But a lot of cataloguing has been done. Charles Delaunay, another Frenchman, has done the best job with names and dates and players. It's called *The Hot Discography*. It has faults, like all pioneer work, but it exists and it lists.

"The avant garde boys didn't do much damage and they saved a lot of old records from the ash-can. The Hot Record Society published a magazine around 1938, *The Rag*. The United Hot Clubs of America did a lot to separate the hot from the sweet schools, to explain who had started it and who had swiped it. There were a raft of books published about jazz history, a lot of them bad, some of them very good as to facts and dates and names; a few were readable, the rest mostly for the fanatics—so packed with names, dates and written either in professor's English or reporter's prose that you had to love the stuff a lot to wade through it. But it all helped, it all made the subject serious because people are impressed by the printed word about anything."

"The white players did their best, in some cases, to keep the ideas of New Orleans jazz going. Up until 1942, Lu Watters' *Yerba Buena Jazz Job Band* played around at the Dawn Club in Market Street in San Francisco, making records, using King Oliver's instrumentation. In 1946, they were back in business again still working on New Orleans jazz. The interest in jazz was real and even the goons couldn't keep it from staying around.

"Dr. Stephen Wise, a square, said, 'When America regains its soul, jazz will go.' Charles Wakefield Adams said, 'Jazz is not spiritual,' but he is said to be tone deaf. Doc Damrosch agreed. 'Jazz is caricature . . . vulgarisms.'

"But there were other voices in other rooms. Leopold Stokowski said, 'Jazz is here to stay . . . Already its vigor, its new vitality is beginning to manifest itself.' Maurice Ravel added, 'Jazz is the only original contribution America has yet made to music.' And Sergei Rachmaninoff said it right out, 'The seed of the future music of America lies in Negro music'."

"Jazz has done a lot of things that make it amazing to Frenchmen who have written its history, often without knowing what true jazz was in its original forms; then later they have gone back and tried to fill in the gaps. Their work has always been good, yet unreal; just as ours would be if we tried to write a serious book on French underworld jargon. Serious jazz has even been tried in Rome in 1950, and there is talk of jam sessions on the Island of Mallorca—but this is all *chi-chi,* some of it by serious students, most of it just fashionable by-play."

"The dictionary definition of jazz hasn't gone far—just helped foul up something that is both a composing and performing art. Enough time has passed so we can say that jazz has cycles, but we haven't yet seen it spiral much. From the cultural anthropologist, from the aesthetic critic, the nylon-towered philosopher we have gotten little beyond high-sounding corn. The best reasons have come, so far, from Basin Street and the Ozark Hills, from Chicago's South Side, from The Stroll in Harlem; and like the men who saw the nailing on the Cross, the true facts should have been enough to put into history.

"It is not true, as some critics say, that the nucleus of jazz has remained constant. It has become a small expanding universe. These critics would like it to be constant, but actually like any living art, it changes—or should change—as it grows. That its growth seems slow to us is something that will not be apparent to the listener a hundred years from now. But as to what jazz is, that will always be a question to us here, now. It could be the feel of a speeded-up tempo while still keeping the old tempo, or a collective improvisation, rhythmically integrated; it certainly can be answered the easy way by calling it syncopated syncopation."

"Evaluation of jazz is not hard if you avoid trying to decide if it's good solid folk-art, or really the platform of a great new musical art, as we shall not even try to answer. We can treat jazz as an art without screwing it into the place it will finally take, but not in our time. For the thing is still a baby, and in no baby can you tell what the nose and features will look like to that old devil posterity, who upsets every generation's ideas of its own smartness."

"As in all art, changes occur in jazz. We have seen them and they haven't, as yet, amounted to much. There is no real aesthetic standard set for jazz—that art of making spontaneous notes and chords, extemporaneous rhythms all set in the art of improvisation. We can judge it only by our personal reactions to its freshness, its profundity and its skill. We have based too much, so far, on mere skill, been taken in by surface freshness and neglected true profundity, because every man is his own boss as to what is profound in jazz, and what ain't.

"So-called eternal truths mean nothing any more to the critic, for we have seen the absolute in our time riddled like a chicken-thief. The absolute has been destroyed, and the trick of beating old dogmas with a new stick will not work. There is no one way of ascertaining today the value of a work of art, a godhead, a history, or a science. The atom is really in flux and time and space and can no longer be pinned down the way our grandfathers planned it. They knew the true God, the greatest novels, the only pure morals—their own. Their coin of sureness has no spending values in our shops. We no longer insist that all art must have a declarable end, and must have a definable means to get there; we know, now, that this is the sterile bunk of the academy. We can only judge our personal reactions to freshness, profundity and skill. And we put too much trust in just skill. The surface of masterpieces pleases us more than the poet's skull beneath the skin. We are patsies, also, too often to only the intuitions and tensions that warp and woof the surfaces of art. Aristotle means something else by intuition when he defined the stuff as that which occurs when the mind is in direct contact with itself (that's jazz in its purest form—the mind in the contact with itself).

"To this add the material; the slave-world, the grafting-on of white and European music, the tunes and chords that are jazz, also the skill, the accuracy with which this is made into music."

Lulu always wants to do
What we boys don't want her to
Don't bring Lulu!
I'll bring her myself . . .

When you talk about what jazz is going toward, you're talking a lot about Lulu. Jazz is doing a lot of things the boys don't like, but if they have to live with it, they'll bring Lulu—not the long-haired boys from Europe, or from the Curtis.

It's been hard work only up to now to live the history of jazz, and its people and its music, but now when the future is pretty close it's got to be said as simply as it can be said, but with no idea that what is said is anything but ideas, ideas based on a lot of study and talk and thinking. The answers don't have to be right, but they are answers or, at least, as much answers as we can now make.

All 'round the water-tank
Waitin' for a train.
Left my gal in the mountains
Left her standin' in the rain . . .

"That's about where jazz is left—standin' in the rain, waitin'. . . . It's safer that way. Because there never may be a real new jazz—more-or-less orderly progress of jazz upward. Art forms die out and get no place lots of times. Glass-painting, copper-plate writing, the poster, and lots of others started as folk art and could have become something, but they died out. You start with what you have and go on doing your best.

Fox, he got a bushy tail;
Possum's tail is bare.
Rabbit got no tail at all
But only a tuft of hair . . .

"Jazz is still a tuft of hair—real, colorful; maybe it can't grow bigger (but the whale got into the water and grew a hell of a big tail). And you can't ever look back over your shoulder and write off what was done in the jazz past. It's still there to hear. Mary Lou Williams' piano, playing *Swing For Joy,* Cootie Williams' horn, playing *Jazz Lips* and *Shout 'em Aunt Tillie,* Teddy Wilson on the ivory keys doing *Blue Lou,* George Whittling's set of skins in *At Sundown* and *Carnegie Jump,* Chick Webb's own drums in *That's My Home, Go Harlem,* or *Who Ya Hunchin'?* Fats Waller doing *Numb Fumbling* and *Viper's Drag* and *Spring Cleaning,* Frankie Trumbauer's alto and tenor sax work in *A Good Man Is Hard To Find,* Frank Teschemacher's clarinet in *Jazz Me Blues,* Art Tatum's piano in *With Plenty of Money and You,* Muggsy Spanier on the cornet in *The Lonesome Road*—and a lot more. All of those that have remained on recordings, some still in good shape, some just ghosts found worn out, with the grooves half-gone in old flats, in junk-shops and ash-cans.

"They laid it down with Buddy Bolden and King Oliver and Bix, and a lot of others, a solid foundation on which, you would think, they could build and go on building. But the new jazz has been slow coming. You can't get angry about it because you can't cut art like cookies and bake them in batches. Music you make real when it's slow-baked, when it's tried out and fitted to the needs of the player and the listener; when it's made to last, made to lead to something else." That kind of art there is never too much of around. Sometimes it suddenly sprouts out of thick streams for a little time, like Elizabethan poetry, Russian novels, Italian painting, but it doesn't last. The great makers die off and when their stuff hardens, a lot of good people with only talent come along and try to keep on building. That's why the new jazz is so slow in coming.

The new jazz is still only hinted at. So we can talk about it as it could be—not as it is. The heroes fall because they are overwhelmed —all art that remains is a victory over destruction. Yet one needs only to make music to have a destiny.

The true art of any era is a deep and broad account of the color and content of the individual and his shapes and sounds for living. The artist has a way of looking at things; in words he sees and criticizes man; in music he senses and appraises his destiny. He knows chords are little mirrors of a time and place and cannot be grasped, understood imaginatively without a knowing of the inside and outside of their contents. Glib generalities in art are the result of ignorance of relevant particularities. Real creators are terrible folk when gripped by great passions. We can only see them clearly when the flames of their creation have burned down a little. Most men fire and char too easily, but the real artist walks the hot coals hunting for the secrets—finding sometimes that man is abstract, and his idea and fate nonabstract.

Ordinary people want popular music in its mere essence, the artist wants it with its content. Basic to great jazz is a harmony of shapes, yet broken often by dissonance—sometimes with blaring, repeated discords. These crescendos rise to a climax, followed by a diminuendo of color and form—another crescendo, another climax. Some see this as the future of jazz—some think it can never be a great art.

The modern jazzman hunting new forms is a thinker. The modern artist is not a gravedigger, an opener of tombs—he overcomes death and returns things to life. His Lazarus is a living work of art.

"You can't find in real life anything—he feels—that will last a lifetime, you find it only inside yourself—something essential and profound. It's something that leads from joy to pain, from pain to illusions, from there back to the pursuit of living . . . and it is *there,* inside, that art is shown as the only species of eternity that means anything—at least, for the artist.

"Everything that is now colorless and intangible will become solid and firm once you admit the inner reality the jazzman feels. The artist fixes and nails things together that stop time as it swings by and he finds again, explores and gives back to the world aspects of the eternal—and so artistic salvation comes to you, and from you to a lot of human beings."

In the mess of modern living no absolute world appears again. "Some find a sort of absolute in a godhead, and mumbo-jumbo—but for the artist, music *is* a religion—always has been, because it communicates to human endeavor the truth which a few minds refine with great agony."

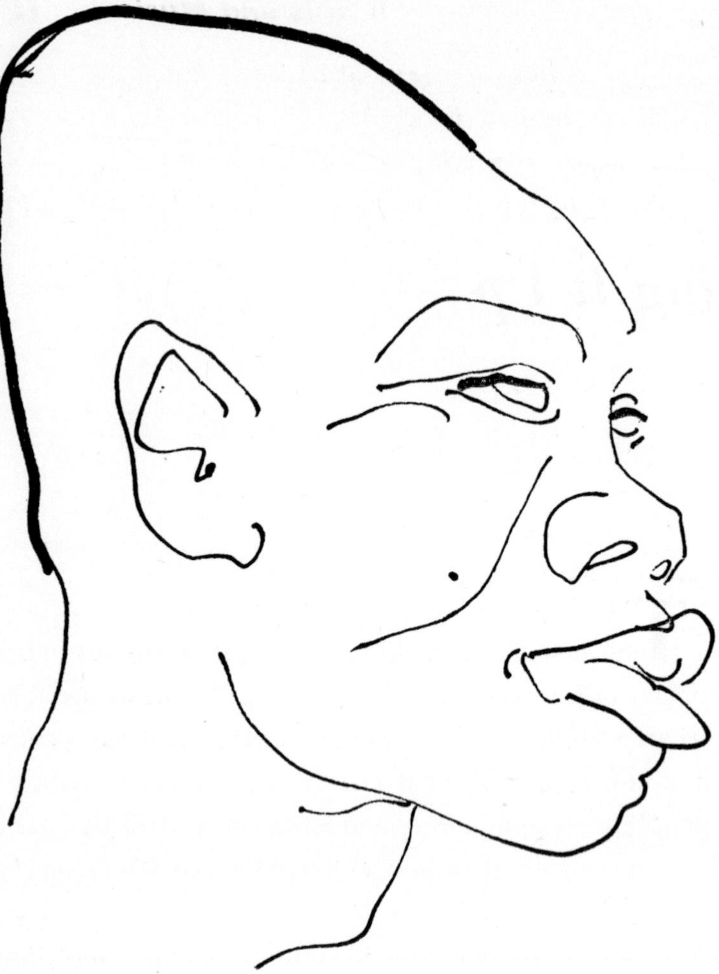

Rich folks worries 'bout trouble
Poor folks worry 'bout wealth.
I don't worry 'bout nothin'
All I want is my health . . .

Six long months done pass
Since I slept in a bed.
And I ain't et a square meal
Of vittles in three weeks.
Seems like money thinks I'm dead—
But I'm satisfied,
Yes, I'm satisfied . . .

SATISFIED

Chapter 23

Summing It Up

The history of religion is not just religious experience, as the history of jazz is not just the sound of the music itself, but in jazz there is an adding up where words and facts and dates count.

"It comes down to this—that jazz, or any art-form—is only as great as the people who come along and work on it. And jazz has always been the names of the people who played it—or who sang it or wrote it.

"It's very new, it's done a lot, and could have done more. Some of it is the work of a race and a people; it's the music of most of the lonely, the sad, the happy and the hopeful. When the right people come along, who can do better with it, they will do it. Meanwhile, you can only wait. . . . There must be a kid with a horn playing alone, dreaming of what he can do and maybe he'll be the Bach, the Mozart of the new jazz, or more likely he'll die in an alley of bad likker, freeze to death with nothing to show for it but some scar-tissue. Maybe some other kid is mooning over a battered piano, hoping to get into a sweet band and make enough money to buy a cut-down jalopy, and get a girl—but maybe he'll begin to play music that will grow with his years and when he's mature, it will be the new jazz, and confound all the critics and please all the listening cats. If people can't do it, nothing else can. Music is the great drug, the true opium of the people.

I was comin' down State Street,
Comin' down Main.
I was lookin' for de woman
What use cocaine . . .

"Jazz is not a primitive thing; it's a folk thing still, and folk things change when the folk go. The ideas and talk and life of the wagon-trains and the forty-niners mean little to their modern great grandsons except as material for poor motion-pictures and phony legends. So jazz had to change as time passed. For by the end of the twenties, almost all the important jazzmen had been born, had died, or were still playing—but no new young giants were coming up.

"You have trouble counting off a dozen jazz players and music makers since 1930 who are as creative as the pioneers, men like Louie Armstrong, Jimmy Harrison, Buddy Bolden, King Oliver, Tommy Ladnier, James P. Johnson; the list could go on for a long time.

"The young folk all try and feel it, but they're not producing all the progress the early men made in the music in their time. Maybe it's because they didn't hear the pioneers themselves, didn't grow up with the blues, the hard time, when it was coming alive and stirring itself and becoming great. But there isn't any proof that lack of troubles is what makes later jazz show so little progress. Neither is the idea that most jazzmen today can read orchestration, and went to school and got educated some, a reason for jazz not moving fast enough. Ignorance, poverty and dirt are the three most over-rated forces for making good art ever produced by fat-belly critics trying to find out what makes art tick. The answer is most likely that a new art form starts when burning men set each other on fire, and produce a new thing, shiny and red-hot, and then as it cools it takes a long time to hammer it into the shape of a full and lasting art. These could be the long days of hammering, of slowly pounding, making a lot of mistakes and yet getting in a few good blows on to what the final shape, the steel-hard shape may be."

The pioneer efforts remain in many cases. You can taste the giants before the end of the twenties by listening to Bessie Smith sing *Sobbin' Hearted Blues;* Louie blowing *All The Wrong You've Done;* Chippie Hill singing *Pratt City Blues;* Louie again doing *Skid-Da-Da-Dat* or *Struttin' With Some Barbecue,* or *Muggles;* Buster Bailey's clarinet and Bessie Smith in *Jazzbo Brown From Memphis Town;* Count Basie's piano, *Doggin' Round;* Ray Bauduc's drums in *New Orleans Twist;* the sax of Sid Bechet in *House Rent Blues* or *Shake It And Break It* or *Lay Your Racket* or taking up the clarinet in, say, *Perdido Street Blues.*

You can hear the pioneers in Bix Biederbecke's cornet playing *Singin' The Blues;* Bill Benford's tuba in *Shoe Shiner's Drag* or *Boogaboo;* Bunny Berigan's horn do *Nothin' But The Blues;* Leon Berry's tenor-sax in *Stealin' Apples.* Barney Bigard's *Harlem Flat Blues.* Bennie Carter's sax in *Six Or Seven Times;* Eddie Condon's banjo in *The Minor Drag;* Baby Dodds' drums rattling in *Too Tight* and *Willie The Weeper,* and Johnny Dodds' clarinet in *I'm Goin' Away To Wear You Off My Mind, Weary City,* and *Brush Stomp.*

Then there is Bud Freeman's sax in *The Eel* and *China Boy;* Lionel Hampton's vibraphone in *Buzzin' Round With The Bees;* Coleman Hawkins' sax in *Rhythm Crazy* and a lot of others. But this isn't a book made up of lists and names. It is trying to find out what the new jazz can be and how it will come about. And there aren't too many answers.

In jazz, some see the classic and the romantic, the old and the new, and agree with Goethe:

> I call the Classic the healthy, and the Romantic the sick. The moderns are not romantic because they are new, but because they are weak, sickish and sick.

Are the ancients Classic because they are old? No—but because they are fresh, strong, happy and healthy.

We have read that before, and it's nonsense. The classic babies had once been moderns, romantic ones too, only old age had made them classic in Goethe's mind, and in the minds of some jazz critics.

"What are the limits of jazz? Are there limits? It remains, in most jazz, that the actual performance is in itself important, so that other music must accept or reject a playing style that is significant in itself. The academic composers with their melodic lyricism often feel the weakness of their work when compared to the strength of hot jazz, and they react in two ways: they try to take over some of jazz's vitality, or they reject jazz as the howling of half-dressed savages. This solves nothing." The scalar, rhythmic and harmonic power of jazz will haunt the house of music a long time. Just what they can do with it will have to be answered when the men arise (or even the man) who can create with it without moaning that it lacks the restraint of the older art-forms. It certainly has form—but to compare it to old churches, Greek architecture and Russian novels is going by old critical standards that no longer mean a lot to our times.

We no longer really believe too much, since Hitler and the atom-bomb, in the perfectability of human aspiration that is behind such great music as the symphonies of Beethoven. Mark Twain's "damn human race" has let itself down too often for the modern maker of music to put too much faith in any too perfect ideal.

"An art that is close to the dance (as jazz is) is close to the simple rock-bottom things of life. The killer-diller arrangements are part of the pace of living . . . and even Mozart and Bach were pretty close to the physical life of their times (which doesn't mean to say that they are close to jazz)."

"The antagonism between the jazz music and the lovers of the older form is proper, for nobody rigidly set in time likes to see the old

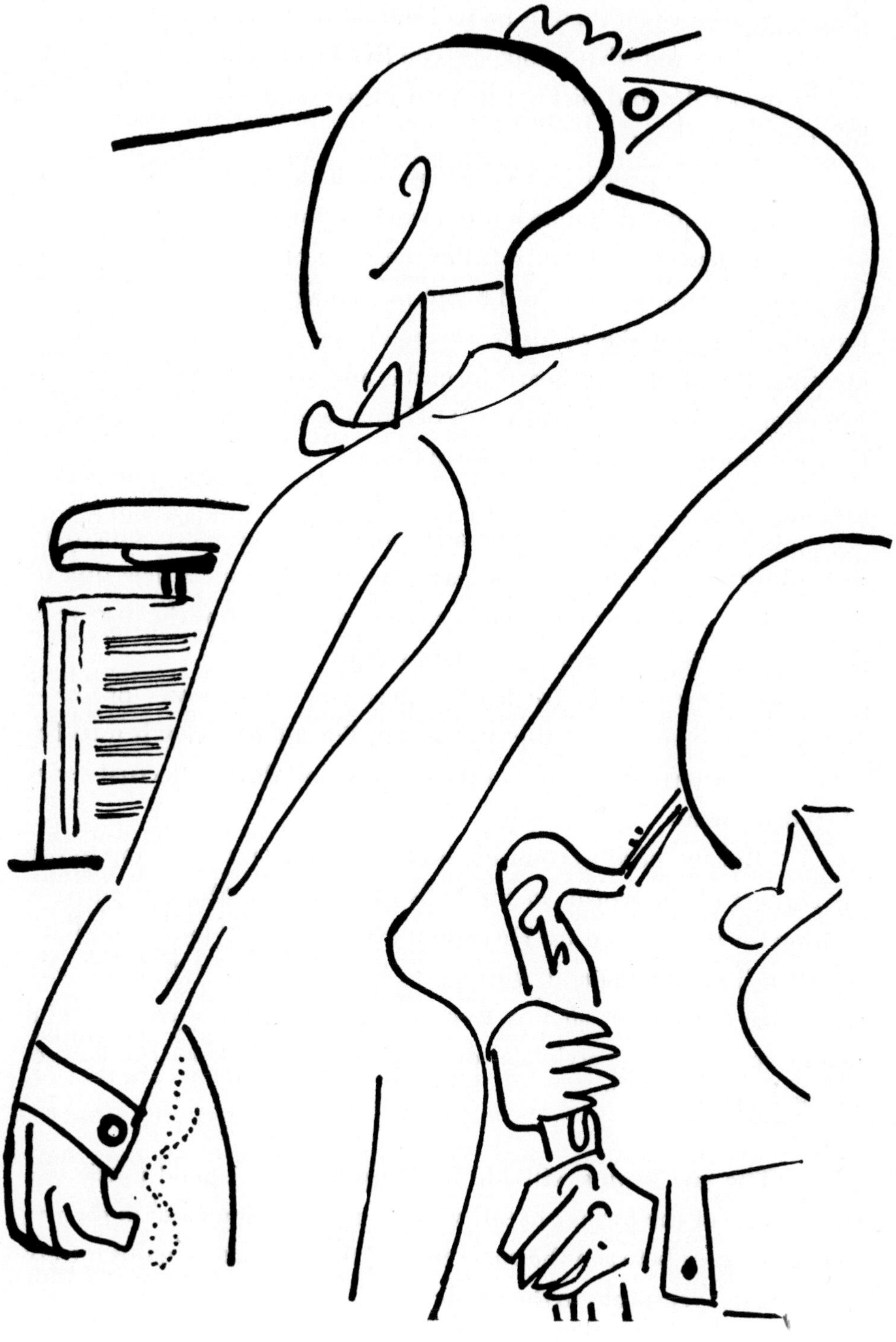

things go; also, when there is no real standard of setting up rules as to what is real art and what is folk-art, you live in an exciting world, making its own rules and picking its own ideas—and some people don't like to live that way.

"The jazz player isn't very high on the scale of life as to education and background, but he is often working for a new ideal in music" —a closer view of truth and a fuller meaning of life, trying to absorb them into his music—not in Theophile Gautier's "art for art's sake" formula, but to make of his work something always new yet always creative. Jazz drops overboard formulas and the mere antique, for it is willing to face the difficulties of original work, rejecting easy solution and going beneath the surface of things.

Cezanne was talking like a jazzman when he said: "One does not substitute one's self for the past; one merely adds a new link to the chain. . . . Art is not a servile copying of objects but the discovery of a harmony among numerous relationships."

It is here that the battle of modern jazz will be won—or lost— in the subordination of subject to motif. For all art today is torn between the pattern of violence of the savages, and the intellectual codes of civilized man.

"But the need to combine both is no longer a searching in the far corners of the world, in the halls of museums. Modern music is waiting for the jazz genius. He cannot avoid it; it will be around him, it will roll on the floor, it will beg to be understood." But only the true artist will see it—it was Renoir who first saw the truth: "The primitive and savage style can draw its inspiration from the flowers in one's own garden."

The jazz genius will add it all up to this: A good music is a transposing of the forms of reality to an inner feeling close to theory, so that it hangs between the concrete and the abstract, remains purely personal and yet speaks to the whole world.

As jazz progresses, the external, the phenomenal world, becomes merely the peg, an illusion, onto which the artist hangs other illusions, with which he creates or destroys our own visions or ideas.

Most other modern music is tied to Euclid's now sterile artistic shapes, repeating a universe of worn-out thought. But the jazzman is a free agent; he can shift gears from that which is outside to that which is inside and not be hampered by discarding nature's suggestions completely. The world is opened like a ripe peach, it splits apart like cell-forms reproducing, multiplying like tadpoles to him.

His forms, his tones when concentrated and distilled, become his own world which he offers freely to us. The only thing his music demands is believers in this inner world—this world that does not directly condemn or acquit; it relates a sympathy with all that lives, stirs, feels. It reconciles us—as all good music does—to reality.

Hush, hush, somebody callin' my name.
Hush, hush, somebody callin' my name.
O, my Lord; o, my Lord,
What shall I do?
I'm so glad trouble don't last always,
I'm so glad . . .

Note on Sources

In February 1944 I had a show of the first jazz drawings and paintings I was to exhibit in public. This was at the Esther Robles Gallery, in Los Angeles. A collector of both paintings and jazz recordings asked me to go to New Orleans and do further paintings on the subject. I took with me a sketchbook I had filled in 1935 with jazz scenes and people, and as I worked I began to compile this into a form that became the basis for this book. In 1944, I began to tape-record a great many talks with old jazzmen. The results with the first machine were poor, but a year later I went back and, with a friend to run a new recording machine, wound up with some tapes of historic value. This book is the result of many years of working with these tapes and my sketchbooks and paintings.

The Buddy Bolden material was hard to come by, and a great deal of it was tied up with legend. I even have doubts that many of the photographs shown of him are really the man. He may have made the first jazz recordings around 1912, but if any still exist, I have been unable to trace them. We badly need a fully documented book on Bolden.

In 1936, while working on a radio show with Red Nichols, I first met many of the early Harlem jazzmen. My notebooks from this period have furnished some of the Harlem text here used, but a great deal was gotten many years later. Many records of old band bookers and blues singers' agents still exist, and are now in the hands of collectors. I have used such records, as I pointed out in the Introduction.

In ten years of working in and out of New Orleans I had the luck of interviewing a great many now-forgotten jazzmen just before they died, or became senile. The Storyville background has been so distorted and changed around to fit romantic concepts of the period that I have used only actual records of the period—newspapers, private journals, and a few publications in print, to check what I was told about it.

Chicago is well documented as to its history since the turn of the century, although a great deal of myth had to be gone through to get even one major fact cleared. In my talks with the Chicago School of jazzmen I had to discount the rosy memory of now-aging people.

There is a great deal of King Oliver material, but no major book about him has yet been written. His letters need to be collected and the yellowing files of old magazines searched more carefully than I was able to.

The Louis Armstrong story is still being told, and he himself has just published part of his life story. I have much more material than I have given here, but I have, I think, indicated his place in the full history of jazz.

The jazz language needs a whole book for itself, and in this book I have not touched on the erotic content of the talk; that belongs in another kind of book. I had intended to have a chapter on the jazz notes and tones and how they have carried over into modern poetry and prose, but it was decided to leave this out as being beyond the limits of this book.

There is a great deal on the philosophy of jazz and its thinkers that should be in print, but in the end it was decided to bring all this down to the final chapter, "The Summing Up."

This leaves me with about a hundred cases of material that could not be put into this book; much of it is of value to the serious historian of jazz. It is my hope to compile another book some day soon from this material.

The notebooks and tape recordings of the original material that went into the making of this book are now on loan to the New World Jazz Society, which is preparing a Complete Dictionary of Jazz.

Index of Names

THE REAL JAZZ OLD AND NEW was set in Baskerville and Bodoni types and printed on Garamond Text. Composition and presswork was done by the WILLIAM BYRD PRESS, INC.; SHREVEPORT ENGRAVING CO. made the engravings and the binding was done by MOORE & COMPANY.

LOUISIANA STATE UNIVERSITY PRESS

The Real Jazz Old and New

By Stephen Longstreet

More nonsense has been written about jazz than any subject except, perhaps, romantic love. This book aspires to add as little nonsense to the subject as possible. It lets the jazzmen tell their own story in their own words. It sets down in words and drawings what has so far failed to appear in books about jazz: the sound and smell of the real thing, the mood and marrow, the pleasure and ache of the jazz world.

And the people who are in it. The great and the unsung figures of the Stone Age of Jazz are now mostly dead or dying off fast, and the things they had to say about jazz and its inventors are important and worth recording.

The Real Jazz Old and New is a collection of their words, their voices and opinions, and is told in their language.

It is *not* a history of jazz in the formal sense, cluttered with names and dates, and it is certainly *not* an appraisal of jazz from the critics' viewpoint.

It *is* a serious study, and it treats jazz—from Dixieland to the West Coast School—in a serious way. But, like jazz itself, it remains in its own backyard and gets some of the fun and fine feeling from the deep blue of jazz itself.

Included as an important part of the real jazz story are many of the drawings and paintings of jazz life and jazzmen the author has made in the jazz joints of New Orleans, Chicago, New York, and Los Angeles.

For students and jazz historians this book presents material that can nowhere else be found, and for lovers of jazz it tells a great story in a new and exciting way.

About the Author

Author, playwright, artist, and critic, Stephen Longstreet has worked off and on for over ten years on this book, interviewing famous and down-and-out jazzmen alike in their native habitats. His many works include *The Beach House*, one of the best novels about Hollywood; *High Button Shoes*, the Broadway musical that received the *Billboard* Award for the best play of 1948; the popular motion picture *The Jolson Story*, and the best-selling travel book *The World Revisited*. His last book, *The Boy in the Model-T Ford*, is now being readied for movie production. Longstreet was recently appointed editor-in-chief of the New World Jazz Society's projected *Complete Dictionary of Jazz*.